The 12 Dimensions of a Service Leader

Manage Your Personal Brand for the Service Age

Po Chung

with

Ran Elfassy

First Edition

ISBN 13 digit: 978-0998166575

ISBN 10 digit: 099816657X

Lexingford Publishing

New York   Hong Kong   San Francisco   Ottawa

www.lexingfordpublishingllc.com

Preface

Welcome to The 12 Dimensions of a Service Leader, one of the key parts from the Service Masters Editions catalog. Before diving into the material, I will explain why we wrote this series and how this book fits into it.

To begin with, let's go back a few centuries, when farmers started using advances in technology to include practices that would eventually lead to manufacturing. Through world trade, particularly over the past three decades, manufacturing moved to Asia, first to Japan and then China and other developing countries. The result is that advanced economies are shifting more toward service.

In order to appreciate the context of these works, let's put a philosophical spin on it to understand how a book's content is time dependent. Even if books themselves last for years, the ideas and words are stacked in ways that take time to write and then take time to read. A book also fits within a writer's lifetime and that author's personal 'timeline'. Understand where a book came from, how it came to be, and how it fits with respect to other works and you begin to appreciate its content. For these reasons, I'm prefacing all my books in the Service Masters Editions with this message.

From the day I was born in Macau in 1943 until the time I was inspired to co-author and draft *The First 10 Yards— The 5 Dynamics of Entrepreneurship* and *how they made a difference at DHL and other successful startups*, my experience fed the momentum that would result in the Service Masters Editions. Since we live our lives looking forward but make sense of our experiences by looking back, it was only after I was well along the path of service leadership that I realized how all of this work fits under the Service Leadership banner.

For example, the first edition of *The First 10 Yards* didn't explain entrepreneurship under the light of service leadership. That would come out after publishing the first edition. However, my co-author Dr. Saimond Ip and I have since updated the book to reflect its rightful place within the Service Leadership domain. Although *The First 10 Yards* was originally written to help budding entrepreneurs, we explain how entrepreneurs are – essentially – service leaders to the people in their startup. We've also added more thoughts on specific needs relevant to a service organization.

I now have a much greater appreciation of how economies are trending towards greater and better service, and why service leaders are the crucial ingredient for organizational success. The best jobs are service jobs, and the best roles are service roles. Even in a multinational manufacturing company – producing anything from micro hinges to the latest electric car or smartphone – how people are organized, managed and led fall under service leadership.

One way of thinking about service is that it's the energy that exists between two people. If that energy delights and inspires, elevates and informs, then this is because of superior service leadership. Unlike a product, which brings excellence to people wherever it is, a service is co-created as the energy between the service giver and receiver. Service leadership is one-to-one, between people. Even if the service organization provides service to millions around the world, the service moment and that service energy is exchanged from one to another. Under service leadership, my co-authors and I stress that a leader is someone who has followers, and good service leaders attract their followers through trust and respect. Just as no consumer would willingly choose a defective product or a product with a 'fatal flaw', people would eventually be repelled by a leader with a critical defect.

Whether an organization is a home, school, hospital, hotel, station, airport, or office, under the Service Leadership glossary these are service 'habitats'. Services are usually organized within habitats and do not happen in isolation from the greater system we call the 'service ecosystem'. Across habitats and ecosystems, the most competitive service and the health of that service is best when the people respect the service principles and rules that support the foundation of that habitat or ecosystem.

I passionately believe that superior service is how we help others when we are at our best. This is us in our whole, multidimensional selves, there to connect with others in ways that last and make a difference. Through these books, not only do I hope that you will be a better service leader at your office, home and everywhere in between, but I hope that they will offer new ways to feel happier and more fulfilled.

Thank you for including me on your journey.

Po Chung
Hong Kong

Po Chung dedicates his work in the Service Masters Editions to future generations.

He extends his deepest gratitude to his beloved wife, Helen, their three daughters, Yana, Anca and Yangie, their son-in-law, Eric, and two grandsons, Connor and Trevor, for their much-needed, enduring support and immense encouragement throughout the long writing journey. Their trust is greatly appreciated.

Po Chung

For Delian and Cadence – we are the lucky ones.

Ran Elfassy

About the Authors

Po Chung co-founded DHL International in 1972 and he is Chairman Emeritus of DHL Express (HK) Ltd. He is also the Chairman of both The Hong Kong Institute of Service Leadership & Management, and The Good Life Initiative Limited. He has been a thought leader and keynote speaker on entrepreneurship, leadership, and corporate culture at conferences around the world. He is the co-author of *25 Principles of Service Leadership*, *Service Reborn*, *The First 10 Yards – The 5 Dynamics of Entrepreneurship and how they Made a Difference at DHL and other Successful Startups*, and other books.

Ran Elfassy has known and helped Po Chung since 2006. He has worked across many sectors in various communications-related roles, delivering advisory services for multinationals and smaller firms across North America and Asia Pacific.

"Intelligence plus character – that is the goal of true education."
Martin Luther King Jr.

"Real leadership, in nations or companies, comes from respect from the top to bottom and bottom to top of the organization."
Simon Sinek

Table of Contents

We Are in the Service Age

For most of our lives we aren't *makers* but *providers*. We give our energy and knowledge to the people we know and we receive other people's energy and knowledge in return. Put another way, we usually relate to one another with what I call a service provider's mentality. Yet the way most people behave and are managed or led in their professional lives has roots in what could be called the manufacturing mindset - roots which date back to the Industrial Revolution.

For a few hundred years, manufacturing drastically changed and dictated the landscape for professional standards and behaviors. To succeed in manufacturing, there are rules and invisible pillars that define how people perform and act toward one another, such as those we find common to production lines the world over. The manufacturing mindset that lasted for generations and still lingers to this day is what was used to get things done efficiently and offer direct benefits, but all that is different now, given that we in the advanced economies have entered the Service Age. For most of us, we would do better to leave manufacturing in the past and focus on returning to a service mentality.

One core message in this book is that if you want to stay relevant and remain competitive in today's advanced economy, you need to shift from the command-and-control manufacturing mindset to the service mentality. This is necessary as societies move from mainly industrial production to service, something we're seeing around the world. Life – maybe even civilization itself – is based on people providing services to one another. Since manufacturing was the driving force for economies for so long, its mentality took over and the principles of service fell behind. Now that we've moved beyond the manufacturing mindset that was born in the Industrial Age, we have the post-Industrial, *Service Age*. Moreover, the use of the term 'service' with regard to this book has a specific meaning that shouldn't be confused with the popular use of the word. When most people think of service, they typically think of things like customer service and service-sector jobs like those in the hospitality industry. Although these are good examples of service, our meaning here is less specific, yet more profound. We will get deeper into this discussion in the coming pages, but it is critical to first point out that service for our use here refers to any activity that involves the energy and relationship created by two or more people in order to get something done. I will argue that the most competitive service systems and organizations are the kinds that work best under *distributed* leadership. By distributed leadership, I mean where two or more people are together and the decision-making or authority can be shared across the group. This key distinction around distributed leadership helps to clarify why some service moments or organizations work better than others.

Before we continue to describe what I mean by service, distributed leadership, the Service Age, or the differences between manufacturing and service, I want to put this book in the right context. Ran and I are committed to helping you move forward in life and it's important that you start by understanding why and how we got here.

This guide came about a few years after I committed to helping bring General Education courses to Hong Kong's undergraduates. At the time, all eight of the city's universities agreed to add a GenEd stream for their students, but the issue was that they didn't have the knowledge or experience of how to teach the material in the most effective way possible. However, I had experienced the power of GenEd while I was in university decades ago. My experience is what then inspired me to help the universities out. Rather than step in with specific GenEd content, I instead helped out by sponsoring more than 20 Fulbright scholars, who came to Hong Kong to help teachers figure out the best way to teach the material. The GenEd courses I took back when I was an undergrad were instrumental in my development, and I hoped the seminars and intellectual development that came from GenEd would help Hong Kong's students as well.

As I see it now, GenEd is what led me to service leadership and service management; not only to understand the content of these domains, but also to understand what was missing in the first place. As my commitment has grown in developing service leadership, I have seen how these programs can deliver real value to our next leaders. Service leadership isn't only for *doing things right*, but also for thinking through and figuring out what is the *right thing to do*. The material in this book is the result of my realization that we can help people get ahead by identifying the principles of service and the dimensions of a service leader.

Unlike many guides that promise recipes for success – such as the skills needed to grow your leadership aura, or what some people call charisma – this guide aims to help you identify and eliminate risks, pitfalls and toxic habits that might lead to failure. To put it another way, this book isn't about telling you what to do to be successful, but it will show you what you need to be aware of and avoid if you don't want to fail.

I firmly believe that when it comes to guiding behavior, it is more pragmatic to avoid the negative than seek the positive. Here is a current, famous example to illustrate this point:

When it comes to large, public and visible companies, Google is certainly among the giants on the world stage. The company has grown so rapidly and left such a profound mark on society that what they do and don't do is on most people's radar. The Google management team includes undisputed corporate leaders who have attracted millions of people based on the quality of who they are and how they serve the global population of Internet users. The company's mission is to "organize the world's information and make it universally accessible and useful," and one of their core values is, "Don't be evil."[1]

It's hard to define what *do good* looks like, even if it can be a powerful aspirational message. But when it comes to a code of conduct or a core value, it's more useful to work under the don't-be-evil directive. This has helped Google get feedback from the market when they do something that ventures into any grey area of operational behavior, because if they do something that is perceived as 'evil' by their customers, they're sure to hear about it pretty quickly. Just as importantly, the don't-be-evil mantra provides a strong internal principle that Google employees follow and can trust. This lends support as they develop new tools, products and services for customers; in fact, this approach goes back to Confucius and even the Ten Commandments. Rather than listing what you need to do to succeed, I will describe what not to do in order not to fail.

Service is like spinning 20 plates while moving between them to keep everything moving and balanced - a dynamic system with many independent moving parts. So it isn't realistic or productive to treat it like it can be frozen in time, like when you stop a production line to fix a local problem. For a service organization to sustain itself, it must deal with each crisis locally, without fear that the organization will come to a halt. In fact, the measure of an organization's excellence can be expressed by how well it manages inevitable, unexpected crises.

We want to stress that everyone who is above the production line is a service *designer*. The principle of design is critical. In fact, the process of becoming a better service leader and creating healthy service habitats essentially comes down to design questions. The principles of service leadership, the 12 dimensions of a service leader, the rules of a service ecosystem (which can't exactly be designed, but must be respected), and the service habitat (which can be designed) are responses, conditions, and insights collected and shared to help you design a healthy service system.

In my previous book, *25 Principles of Service Leadership*, which I wrote with Dr. Art Bell, we described the conditions needed for successful service leadership. In this book, Ran and I offer a more personal checklist of what you can use to improve your own service leadership. This book is really about the *being* side of the service leader, an approach I've used in many classes and seminars. The stress is on the notion that service leadership isn't too concerned with attracting more followers – that kind of cult of personality might be good for some organizations, but not for the kinds of service groups that really stand apart. There is a kind of leadership skill that can look like charisma or charm, but that doesn't address the depth of leadership we aim to discuss here. Instead, service leadership is about cleansing who you are and shedding toxic qualities so that *you don't repel* others.

You will see that my approach is not like what James Kouzes and Barry Posner accomplished with their great work, *The Leadership Challenge*, which they supported by extensive empirical research.[2] This book is more in the spirit of another great guide, by Dale Carnegie, *How to Win Friends & Influence*.[3] Where *The Leadership Challenge* stands out because of the quality of ideas extended and supported from empirical evidence, *How to Win Friends & Influence People* has changed people's lives from a more qualitative approach. I'm not pitting one against the other; I am simply highlighting that the work behind this book offers a pragmatic route on a topic that needs more exploration.

It is my sincere hope and belief that this is by no means the last word on the principles of service and the dimensions of a service leader. For example, there may be more than 12 dimensions, but I doubt there are less than 12 when you thoroughly review what counts. The information and advice offered here are results of my exploration into what it takes to be a truly good service leader, one who has removed or limited the possibility of a downfall because of a personal fault. I'll leave it to the next generation of researchers to build from this point forward.

To highlight what this book addresses even more, the Systems Pagoda in Figure 1 illustrates a model I often use to show the relationship between different systems we face in our lives.

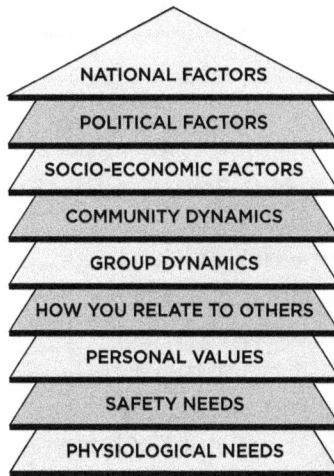

```
              ▲
     ╱─────────────────╲
    ╱  NATIONAL FACTORS  ╲
   ╱─────────────────────╲
  ╱   POLITICAL FACTORS    ╲
 ╱───────────────────────────╲
╱  SOCIO-ECONOMIC FACTORS    ╲
───────────────────────────────
   COMMUNITY DYNAMICS
───────────────────────────────
     GROUP DYNAMICS
───────────────────────────────
  HOW YOU RELATE TO OTHERS
───────────────────────────────
     PERSONAL VALUES
───────────────────────────────
      SAFETY NEEDS
───────────────────────────────
   PHYSIOLOGICAL NEEDS
───────────────────────────────
```

Figure 1 – The Systems Pagoda

The basic premise of the Systems Pagoda is that the bottom level -our Physiological Needs – is survival at its most basic. This includes what is essential to keep our biological state balanced; such as food, shelter, and clothing. Moving up the Pagoda, we find other systems that affect our lives.

This book focuses mainly on the systems of your Personal Values, How You Relate to Others, and Group Dynamics. The other systems are also influences, but for our purposes here, we will deconstruct the three middle systems so they are easier to understand and manage.

This book addresses the critical area of service, the *being* side of yourself as a service leader and how well you are in accordance with the principles of service leadership. As you can see from the Pagoda, there is the Service Ecosystem, which is where we find conditions that are mostly beyond our ability to change or manipulate. Compare this with the Service Habitat, which we can design, influence and change.

To illustrate the point, imagine you're caring for fish in a pond.

You may need to manage – that is, serve – each individual fish, but it's just as important that you serve your total fish population by ensuring the whole pond is healthy – that there's enough to eat, there are no parasites, and the water has the right acidity and oxygen. The pond is like a service habitat, which is what service leaders can directly control through good service design. A service leader also needs to work within the habitat in ways that respect the conditions of the greater ecosystem, which is mostly beyond the service leader's control. For the fish, if the water table in the ecosystem is falling, this will have an impact on the pond. It's not practical to raise the water table for the whole ecosystem, but the effective management of the pond habitat has to respect and follow the conditions set by the ecosystem. In this example, although the ecosystem can't be manipulated as easily, what can be done is we can build a temporary dam or bring more water to ensure the habitat is well maintained.

I hope that as your mindset shifts from manufacturing to service you will appreciate how complex it is. Ran and I aim to help you clear or detox what might corrupt your service leadership potential, now or in the future.

For those who have already been exposed to the model of entrepreneurship I developed with my co-lecturer and co-author, Dr. Saimond Ip, the material in this book is a natural evolution. As we described in our book *The First 10 Yards*, we were prompted to find what was missing in the entrepreneurship models that were available at the time.[4] What we found was a lot of material on the functional side of starting a business, but very little on the being side of the entrepreneur. In *The First 10 Yards*, we covered the primary areas of *Who, What, Who Else, How, and Where* (Figure 2).

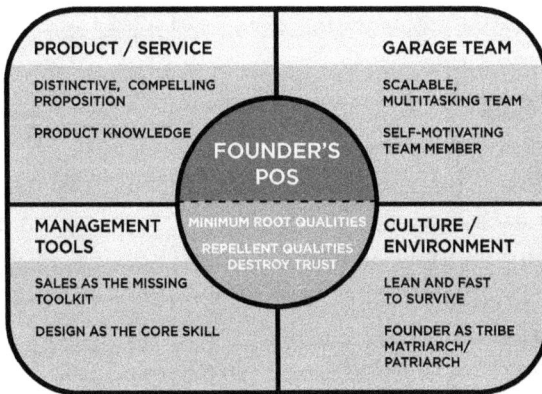

Figure 2. The Five Dynamics of Entrepreneurship Model

What has developed since then is my deeper and broader understanding of service. We urge readers who are interested in entrepreneurial start-ups to review *The First 10 Yards* as it addresses and caters to the entrepreneurial perspective more than my other books. The most important feature relevant to service leadership is around a person's *Personal Operating System* (POS).

To recap what makes up our POS, imagine our brains are like our own personal biocomputers. We collect and process information and can take conscious or unconscious actions. We also use our brains to decide the content of what we say, and to consider the consequences of our actions and other people's reactions to our behaviors. Operating our personal biocomputer is our POS, and, in short, our POS is us.

Another relevant aspect from the analogy is that our biocomputers are connected to the external world by a kind of wireless system. Each of us receives signals and information through our senses and we can then communicate and share with others through words, intentions and actions.

Our POS includes a set of virtues, and these let our POS

smoothly operate and integrate with others. When we come into contact with others, our POS connects with theirs and we influence each other's POS. These networks are everywhere and they exist whenever there are others nearby. This connection also exists when information is disseminated through the Internet, newspapers, memos, television or other media channels. When another person's POS does not connect smoothly with ours (for example, it might contain toxic characteristics) we can feel anxiety, anguish, distraction, frustration and other energy-draining influences.

In the entrepreneurship model, the heart of a start-up is the entrepreneur – especially the *being* side Developing it further, I soon realized that an entrepreneur is at his or her best when acting as a non-toxic service leader. This service leadership – the extension of the POS – is the subject of this book.

With these distinctions made, we can return to the discussion of service leadership. Specifically, we can now focus on the differences between service and manufacturing.

Complicated and Standardized vs. Complex and Variable

Service has to coexist with some level of manufacturing – one without the other doesn't amount to much. The difference is that service delivers the higher-added-value ingredients in the value chain – let's call this the *service value chain*. For example, although a product designer or engineer is valuable in a manufacturing company, the people who are most valuable are those who provide a service within the company. These service providers are the managers, directors and executives who provide leadership services. As for the service sector, transactions are built around 'moments' that are custom-made, individualized and co-created. The salesperson and the customer have a transaction in a moment that is different every time, and even if the final product exchanged through the transaction is the same, each eyeball-to-eyeball service moment can go in almost any direction. This is in contrast to what we see on the production line for mass-produced things, where the end result is a uniform product, undifferentiated from its peers. Product number one is the same as product 1,000,001. In manufacturing, consistency reigns supreme; in service, variability is the constant.

The commitment to a strong service mentality is as true on the national or global level as it is on the individual one. For example, consider Thailand's reputation as the 'Land of Smiles'. This promise is behind the country's reputation as a leader in hospitality, based on a national character that other countries lack or have only in small doses. Japan, for example, has service elements that are strong, but even when the service is polite and deferential, there's an aftertaste of rigidity. This rigidity works against the service mentality needed to really come out ahead. The best service requires room, agility and flexibility to improvise across each service moment, so places like Thailand and Hong Kong in Asia stand out, as do the USA, Canada and the United Kingdom. If flexibility and agility to variable conditions and outcomes is what really makes service different, then the best service leaders have the flexibility to make decisions at the local level, and room to authentically care for others. Care is paramount for excellent service delivery.

In a corporate setting, there's little doubt in my mind that most managers and MBAs still follow models born from the manufacturing sector. MBA schools, after all, were originally created to serve the auto industry; partly to help raise productivity on the assembly line. Although today's economy is dominated by service, the managerial mindset created for manufacturing companies still dominates. I argue that service providers across all industries will be more effective when they shift their mindset from manufacturing to service.

To illustrate the point, consider the lingering 'ghost in the machine' we find in former Communist countries, which are essentially manufacturing-based. Because of the overriding principles of private and professional equality, service relationships fizzled. If everyone's equal, a server has no incentive to go the extra mile for the customer. The push for equality ends up looking like a push towards the average, which in service can mean dropping toward mediocrity rather than rising to excellence. Under these conditions, there's no need or inducement for a server to delight customers. When there's no competition that's fine, or at least not threatening to the survival of the organization; but when competition comes around and forces groups to elevate their standards, the message is, "differentiate through good service or die".

Look at each service provider as an individual to see how service excellence and service leadership happen. In doing so, aim for integrity assurance (as opposed to the quality assurance you look for in products). From my experience in helping grow DHL into a global service leader, I realized that service leadership is perfectly scalable. At DHL, we figured out how to build a network of service leaders and repeated the process again and again. All our service leaders then created new generations of other service leaders. We did this around the world, across different nations and cultures, over and over. Our solution to the problem of training across cultures was to use a master-apprentice model. For example, if it took one week to train a 'generation' of workers, who would then themselves become masters to the following generation of apprentices. This could quickly grow geometrically to scale from one person to several thousand, which we did as we expanded from city to city and country to country. At DHL's peak growth we were expanding by one country every five weeks and one city every eight days. That kind of pace for a service company means you need an especially effective system to train a team. For us, it was through masters and apprentices. This approach is something I believe is the key to creating service leaders. We will revisit the importance of masters and apprentices in Chapter 14, when we will look at the *Leader : Follower* dimension. For now, suffice to say that service leaders are better prepared and groomed if they are apprentices first and later pass on their wisdom as they mature.

Some elements of the Service Age can create businesses that are clearly disruptive to other businesses in the market, as a result of competition. This disruption is the result of growth, evolution and change, and is why we can be confident that service quality can improve over time. This, in turn, is the reason why remaining competitive is achievable.

The differences between the manufacturing and service mindsets depend on a shift in perspective. In manufacturing, people are functional units who complete tasks that can be strictly defined – the more you can limit a procedure to specific tasks, the easier it is to measure, analyze and restructure to increase efficiency. If a procedure is too complex to be done efficiently, it gets split for other functional units to come in and share the workload. These functional units can be anyone, and if that part of the line can be automated, robots will increasingly replace people. In fact, the more you can replace a person with a robot, the better.

Under the service model, however, people are agents whose 'production' and effectiveness rise through empowerment and trust. Their 'humaneness' and engagement plays an important role. Even when you try to capture procedures to analyze and streamline them, there's always the possibility of an unpredictable outcome – variability and change is a constant.

Consider that even if your job is to make something – say you're a carpenter, baker or journalist – your career is still relationship-dependent. Actually, these careers aren't strictly manufacturing ones, since each one is making a 'thing' that has its own character and uniqueness. Although there are manufactured goods in carpentry and baking, many carpenters and bakers are artisans who make things one at a time. Craftspeople merge roles from manufacturing and service into one. The difference, and this is significant, comes from the *industrialization* of behavior.

If we look at true production-line manufacturers, we see that each person on the production line is stripped of the artisan's uniqueness and reduced to strictly-defined functional rules. This is the kind of manufacturing that led to how organizations were managed and designed, and this is not the best approach for the people who make today's organizations and economies thrive.

Under the service model, even if you earn a living by assembling things that others use, you are defined by your interpersonal relations and how you conduct yourself as you serve others. In the Service Age, the era in which we're all service leaders at different moments in the day, we are faced with service opportunities to show our leadership, trustworthiness and ability to work for one another. This means that even on the production line for a large manufacturer, you gain a competitive advantage when you apply the insights from this book and respect the principles of service. I've often seen the rules that work in a manufacturing environment fail to encourage and inspire the strengths that a service leader brings to his or her job. Since life is about offering personal service to the people around us, we can all benefit from upgrading our service leadership skills.

Again, as suggested earlier, many people assume that by

service I'm talking about hospitality or customer service. Although careers in hospitality, like running a B&B or hotel, certainly involve service, the idea of service leadership as I use it here is more comprehensive and at a higher conceptual level. Service includes frontline service providers like a concierge or waiter, as well as lawyers, doctors and even engineers when they're working with clients or managing their teams. Once you move off the production line at a car manufacturer or a company that builds computers, you're a service provider. Management is a service. Leadership is a service. Even being a client, parent or child is a service. Again, everything apart from industrial production lines is a service. Unfortunately, too much management, leadership, and organizational emphasis has been around manufacturing-based operational standards. This emphasis hasn't captured what's needed in our service-based, knowledge economies where people – not things – are at the heart of what we do and why we do it, whatever it may be.

As I mentioned above, the exploration into service leadership is rooted in my years with DHL, which gave me great on-the-ground and global insights. One of the insights I have is that the ingredients of service leadership are the 'dimensions' of a service leader's personal brand. There already is a growing body of work around personal brands, as well as the dimensions of commercial brands. The personal brand of a service leader I refer to demands a holistic approach, and this is what Ran and I developed into our *Service Leadership* seminars. In the seminars, as throughout this book, participants review each dimension of their personal brand in order to improve their skills and service leadership standards. This is crucial because for true service leadership, it's not enough that we have competencies in various skills. For service leadership, we must make a conscientious review of who we are in order to spot and then weed out the negative qualities that could lead to failure. This goes beyond professional training to a kind of self-help toward trouble-shooting the content of who we are, so that we are people whom others will trust, respect and be drawn to follow.

In case you're uncomfortable with the idea of leadership or the suggestion that we can all be service leaders, it could be that the leadership you're thinking of is the classic leader who made it to the top of a pyramid. This leader orders subordinates to "jump" and they are expected to answer, "how high?" and carry out the command. Decision-making is at the top and improvisation is a risk.

That kind of leadership is ideally suited to manufacturing. In service, leaders don't command from the top, because in order to be effective or at a team's most competitive, service people are leaders in a distributed-leadership network. Under this approach to creating the most competitive service leadership, each person must strengthen the 12 dimensions of their service leadership that support their best achievement and being.

With a manufacturing mindset, leadership is top-down and dictatorial. In the service mindset, leadership is distributed and directly tied to the server's level of trustworthiness. Moreover, in service, everyone across the group is faced with decision points that are acted upon at the local level. People get their 15 minutes of leadership every hour, and within those 15 minutes it's the quality of the server's character that establishes trustworthiness and respect, in addition to doing things right, which leads to a service leader's effectiveness by raising his or her ability to engage the full effort of his or her followers.

As I mentioned earlier, the *25 Principles of Service Leadership* lists conditions for service leadership to happen and I'll take a moment to discuss a few. For example, there is the Principle of the 15 Minutes of Leadership, the Principle of Self-and-Other Leadership, the Principle of the Server, and others. From the manufacturing mindset, leadership is characterized by its authoritarian flavor that can be benevolent or not. There are many times when this kind of leadership is preferable, but in a service setting it can directly corrupt either the leader's effectiveness or the company's cohesion. In service, leadership is both top-down and distributed. People are empowered to make decisions at the local level and the decisions are shared across the network for review. Depending on how well a decision fits the company's strategic goals, it is prohibited or repeated.

Another facet of the Service Age is linked to the disruptive innovations brought on by social media. To be fair, DHL began before fax machines, when globalization was still in its infancy. The roots that make international trade and communication so common today were only beginning to break ground back then. One could argue that without DHL, international trade wouldn't have been so efficient.* As a service-oriented company, DHL understood that our people had to be service 'hubs' within our networks. Although social media wasn't around, we needed access points where people 'from here' could reach people 'over there', across boundaries that had previously been too great to cross. Today, as many companies and job seekers are realizing, having social media competence can itself establish a competitive advantage in a market full of noise. Just as approaching service with a traditional command-and-control mindset will set you up for failure, so can a group's social media strategy. Instead of a recipe for disaster, companies and their employees can design distributed leadership across social media platforms using a service mindset. This protects companies from working against the principles of service, and also strengthens a company's activities and positioning across social media.

To help make the most of the being side of service leadership, this book acts as a guide you can use to review who you are through the 12 different dimensions that make you, *you*. This will hopefully raise your awareness of why we need a different approach to managing ourselves if we want to succeed as service leaders.

Life is about providing service to the people around us – a point I will emphasize throughout this journey – and it's in our best interest to be as free from corrupting qualities as we can be. To stand apart and remain competitive, we must constantly improve and strengthen the content of our character and show genuine care for the people in our lives. This guide will take you to each dimension of what makes a service leader effective, and show you ways of improving your chances for success. The approach here isn't to show you how to be in order to succeed. Instead, the method here is to show you that in order to succeed as a service leader, you must manage and find ways to remove the things in who you are that could lead to failure.

---

* It's also worth pointing out that if DHL didn't go around the world, challenging the postal monopoly from country to country, the shipping industry and Internet-based shopping would probably look very different. Not only would it be slower, but companies like Alibaba.com would probably be worth a lot less than they are today.

Chapter TWO

You Are Your Personal Brand

Imagine you're a brand, one that does and means a great deal for the people in your life. This idea and perception of *you* is the essence of your personal brand. This is who you are, what you can do and the service you deliver. After working in the service industry for more than four decades, I'm convinced that improving our personal service to others provides the greatest satisfaction for both giver and receiver. It also improves our ability to be service leaders. By necessity, this review should involve all the facets of what makes us who we are. That is, we must review the 12 dimensions of our personal brand.

By improving our personal brand we can enhance how well we work with others, how well we get ahead in our careers, and how well we behave when a leadership moment crops up. Again, I'm using leadership in the context of where it's distributed, and not the top-of-the-hierarchy seen from the manufacturing mindset. In the Service Age, we all face leadership moments every day and every hour.

This guide will take you through a checklist of your 12 dimensions. For convenience, these can be thought of as the 3-Cs of Leadership, which are your Competence, Character and Care. By taking the complex total system of our personal brand and separating it into subsystems, it's much easier to be thorough. This is a good way to minimize the risk of missing something that might prove critical.

This approach clearly stresses that in service with others, the quality of your leadership is your 'being' side This includes your character, morals, and other facets that most likely haven't been getting the attention they deserve.

No book or training program will stick until we first make the decision to adapt and grow. In order to transform, we must commit to staying on this wonderful, life-changing journey. But like all journeys into the unknown, wrong turns are likely and some turbulence is inevitable. Nevertheless, success is possible as long as the commitment is there. Success is the result of honest effort and, like so many things that have uncertain outcomes, the energy we put in is the energy we get back.

I advise you put all your energy into this program of exploring who you are. At worst, even with no change, you will spend some time getting to know yourself a little better. At best, you will find your Achilles heel and finish radically transformed, prepared to shine as an exceptional service leader. The potential rewards are hard to overstate, be they personal or professional. Since the mission of this book is to help you improve your personal service to others, especially by identifying what to avoid and what can work against you, let's take a moment to review what service is about.

You in the Service Moment

Remember that you are one of your most important customers. Some people find this counterintuitive, so imagine you're about to board a jet and are waiting to fly. If the airline is following standard pre-flight routines, a flight attendant will advise that in the unlikely event of an emergency, if there's decompression in the cabin, for example, first ensure that you have your own breathing mask on before you try to help anyone else. Similarly, although personal service is about caring for others in a service moment, it's important that you get yourself sorted out first.

Second, let's assume there really is a brand called *You*. As I mentioned in the Introduction, personal-brand discussions mostly address the obvious, *Competence : Expertise* dimension. If we think of real products we pick up at the store, like a new faucet, it's easy to understand what an item's *Competence : Expertise* dimension refers to: the qualities of a product that are common to the use of a faucet. There are handles to let the water flow, the stream has to be regulated, and it should come out in a predictable way, with a surface that doesn't let the faucet corrode after a year. In most personal brand discussions, the focus is mostly on the content of a person's *Competence : Expertise* dimension. This captures what we can do, professionally or otherwise.

Added to this, some personal brand discussions include what I call the *Visual : Daily Management* dimension. This is about what we look like, how we come across as a package, and the habits and behaviors that express our image and style.

Let's now broaden this discussion to include items we care about - the brands we are loyal to. Products we care about have more going on than just their functional and visual aspects. This is also true for the personal brand of a service leader, who is someone driven by a mindset with a broader range of traits and standards that go beyond the functional.

Consider a popular product, like your favorite smartphone. We're mostly drawn these days to things including what it can do, what apps are available, if the camera is of a good standard. We are also drawn, however, to the physical design and color, how it feels in our hand, and how stylish it is compared to all the other models out there.

Beyond the obvious *Competence : Expertise* and *Visual : Daily Management* dimensions there are other dimensions. For example, there are the *Social : Relationship*, the *Mental : Intellectual* and the *Spiritual : Inspirational* dimensions.

The *Social : Relationship* dimension includes what owning this brand does to your reputation, or perception of your temperament or social status within your group. The *Mental : Intellectual* dimension represents what kind of person you are on a cognitive or rational level for choosing this phone over others. The *Spiritual : Inspirational* dimension is about how this object connects you to others, and possibly a movement that is greater than you.

If these dimensions look familiar and you've read Thomas Gad's excellent *Branding: Cracking the Corporate Code of the Network Economy*, you will recognize four dimensions he also discussed in his book.[5] I happily encourage people to read Gad. He's as sharp as they come.

Gad developed a model for how to understand branding in the commercial economy. The 12 dimensions of a service leader are different, because they tackle the specifics of how to improve one's personal brand and how well we can succeed in service. Gad identified four key dimensions, and I then applied my own experience to better understand how to succeed as a service leader. This led to identifying 12 separate dimensions. By applying the following checklist to yourself, you can improve who you are, strengthen your personal brand, and establish how well you perform as a service leader. The ultimate goal is to help you become a fully developed and more competent service provider, which in turn can help you feel more fulfilled in your own life.

Let's return to the scenario of buying an everyday item. Again, for many products, we tend to only be interested in the *Competence : Expertise* and sometimes the *Visual : Daily Management* dimensions. For those products, we often don't even care about the brand if the price is right and it serves our functional needs. When we return to something through loyalty, emotions for a brand can run deep and we are sometimes almost blind to everything else on the shelf. At these times we may even judge the people who made the product as special, and the other customers who selected the same we did as enlightened or a cut above the rest. It may not be explicit, but part of a brand's power is to encourage this kind of loyalty and devotion, so that we feel as connected to these other people as we are to the actual product. In other words, we have qualities in common that make it as if we all belonged to the same tribe.

Consider people who buy Vans skateboard sneakers. These shoes are associated with feelings of rebelliousness and being cool. These are shoes for trashing around and ripping it up – not what we normally associate with Adidas or Nike. Look at people who go for Vans versus those who go for Nike, and it's as if each customer self-selects into tribes of those who share similar world views. At the extreme, these people would hardly mix together socially or professionally. Multidimensional brands can influence behavior to intensify loyalties. So Adidas makes athletic shoes, Nike owns a different area of the consumer landscape, and Vans has the street-smart urban antihero. Functionally, Vans limited its product line to target a category that doesn't need to compete against other companies on certain product features, but the brand is a lot more than just the functional aspects of the shoe. In exploring all of this, I realized we can think about service providers – the people – as the brand. For example, DHL is a global courier whose heart is as a service company, while the couriers are the brand. I'm going to refer a lot to DHL, given that I co-founded the international arm of the company more than four decades ago.

In trying to get a fix on the nature and scope of service, I asked myself, what would happen if what I'm really selling is the person behind the service? And what could I learn by defining the dimensions of a top notch service provider? In other words, if I want to promote or simply present myself as a holistic being, what do I need to think about beyond the *Competence : Expertise* dimension?

The most important insight I gained is that the server is the service.

Moreover, that the 12 dimensions of the service leader's personal brand are the aspects of a person's *character* that comes into play when the server is the service.

In order to be at one's best, it's critical that we review who we are so we can see if there is one small defect that could lead to failure. In fact, this is the point of this review.

Small and large defects in our 12 dimensions can easily haunt our efforts, so as service leaders we must be aware of who we are and the quality of our 12 dimensions. This is called the *Anna Karenina Principle*, explored in Jared Diamond's fascinating book titled *Guns, Germs, and Steel: The Fates of Human Societies*.[6] The Principle is named after Leo Tolstoy's great novel, *Anna Karenina*, which begins with the statement, "Happy families are all alike; every unhappy family is unhappy in its own way." Tolstoy's novel explores how qualities unique to a couple can have defects that may eventually bring the relationship to a tragic end. In Diamond's book, he illustrates the principle by asking why so few animals have been successfully domesticated. Although many animals could have been domesticated, if they had one flaw or missing quality in their makeup, it prevented effective domestication from occurring.

A deer, for example, has the flaw of excessive skittishness that makes domesticating it as a livestock too difficult. Some deer populations are domesticated, but they revert to feral behavior easily, especially if they're not closely managed.

With that in mind, suppose someone was always broke or bankrupt; people might get uncomfortable or suspicious of them, and this could prevent this person from being a good service leader. Or suppose someone was always sick; although their loved ones should hopefully stay with them through thick and thin, others may want to avoid that person. The same goes for temperament; what if someone was consistently grouchy? It's likely that people would try to avoid him or her because being with a downer all the time can be exhausting.

I've often seen that if a service leader's character and morals aren't good, people may still want to be around them when they need something, but the person with the toxic character won't get far as a service leader. Each person has their own version of the Anna Karenina Principle – traits that over time may corrupt the ability to succeed as a service leader. After witnessing many examples of this happening, I realized that reviewing the 12 dimensions of a service leader's brand is a checklist that can help avoid the Anna Karenina Principle and increase the chances of success.

I also noticed a big gap that wasn't being addressed in the classroom. When I was teaching entrepreneurship at different universities, I saw that functional competence and skills were being covered, but how to manage service people as a business discipline was missing. Again, the server is the service and the underlying goal of service isn't only to increase the sale of things, but also to sell the actual people who are delivering the service. This is what builds brand integrity, customer loyalty and competitive advantage for long-term sustainability.

Since creating this checklist and refining it with Ran, we have developed a holistic approach for strengthening the dimensions in one's personal brand. Apply this checklist to yourself and you will find what you can do to strengthen your personal brand. You will also find what you need to purge from yourself so that you're managing the Anna Karenina Principle and making the most of every opportunity that comes your way.

I will also take this moment to discuss the issue of self-interest. Although service is the energy we bring into our relationships to help other people, there's a component to the service leadership program that is 'self-centered'. As we shall describe over the coming pages, the project of improving who we are and our personal brand is one that satisfies both how we help others and answer 'what's in it for me?' Even if we come at this as a purely self-centered exercise, or even the complete opposite as a purely other-centered exercise, improving one's personal brand brings rewards across both. The question of 'what's in it for me?' is one that people have been labeling as important to our current generation – the so-called Millennials. Growing up in advanced, knowledgeable economies, and under the pressures of large populations, climate change and an uncertain economic future, the Millennial is supposedly one who is more driven by the self-interested motive posed by the *WIIFM* question. My answer to that is that the current generation of aspiring service leaders have challenges that are unique to them, and that ultimately they will benefit by this program of improved service leadership. What's in it for them is they will be more competitive, and if that isn't motive enough or inspiring enough, then they will simply but profoundly improve by becoming better, more well-rounded people who can make a real difference for themselves and the people in their lives.

Although we could further divide the 12 dimensions into more sub-categories, I doubt any comprehensive list would count less than 12. They all overlap and interact to form a dynamic system, but by separating them we can look at each, adapt as needed and keep refining our service leadership. Ultimately, we will then be able to pinpoint the areas of weakness or potential failure in ourselves and be better contributors to the people in our lives.

To make the dimensions less abstract, let's imagine a newspaper reporter. First, this person must be able to write a coherent story. Then, to be successful, he or she must excel in how to deliver a reporter's service, which includes effectively serving the team at the news desk, the editorial board, interviewees and everyone else involved in delivering the final product of a news story. By the time the article is published, readers only see the printed words – these are the artifacts of the reporter's functional ability to write. Between the lines there is evidence of the 12 dimensions that allow a reporter to successfully get the story published.

The Path to Better Service

There is a path that anyone who wants to succeed as a better service provider can follow. In fact, even if your goal is a romantic one, the insights here can make you even more attractive and a better service provider to your love interest.

Most people think about themselves, at least professionally, through their functional abilities – captured in the

Competence : Expertise dimension; but we all have 11 other dimensions influencing our behavior and how others see us, and the path to success demands that we address our complete selves.

To use a relatively common example, some people don't care much about how they look, but whether they like it or not they're being judged because of something so arguably superficial. This judgment around our visual presentation can deeply influence how people behave toward us, so not caring about our *Visual : Daily Management* dimension can put us at a disadvantage. Quite often, other people make decisions about us even before we open our mouths.

To use a less superficial example, let's imagine a commodities broker who says he doesn't see any practical point in exploring his morals or the content of his character. His goal is to build the volume of funds in his portfolio and he's trying to run a successful business, not a church. Yet, even if he doesn't care about morality or ethics, the other people on his team – junior or senior – may take the perception of his *Moral : Character* dimension very seriously. The time may come when a decision is made because of him that ends up having a direct impact on the company's bottom line. Even if it takes years to address, we must all strive to have some kind of moral compass and authority. How we develop this dimension isn't necessarily something others will even notice after we've done it, but it's definitely something others will notice if our moral direction changes with the winds. When we lose our moral authority, trust in us wavers and people no longer follow us with conviction. They may refuse to work or even simply stop cooperating with us.

I am convinced that life is an entrepreneurial journey and you are the entrepreneur of your life, because no one has ever lived your life before you. So you have to figure it out as you live it. On this journey, if we reduce it to the fundamentals, the business of You is about providing personal services to all the people who are part of your journey. Our personal service is what we extend to our 'personal' customers, suppliers, investors, stakeholders and even competitors. In fact, if you were to write a business plan of the You company, it would be a service business plan. You have suppliers and clients, and the most important stakeholder is you. If you don't take care of yourself, the people in your life can stop being happy with you or enriched by receiving your personal service. One way to care for yourself is by going through the 12 dimensions outlined in this book.

Excellence Through Mindful Persistence

Why should we explore who we are and what makes us tick? Does it really matter, and can this self-improvement produce concrete results? To answer this, I'll review the economic environment that is right in my own backyard.

My years with DHL literally flew me around the world many times over. I've seen the world change from when globalization was an obscure idea to the current age of dizzying interconnection. Over the past few decades, I've also seen my hometown of Hong Kong change from a manufacturing center to a manufacturing lightweight, with nearly all our factories having moved to mainland China and other Asia Pacific countries. The days when we made shirts, radios and anything else that springs to mind are long gone. Now an advanced economy, we're a world-class hub for the service industry where banking, finance, logistics, law and other professions are the pistons in our economic engine. More than 90% of our GDP comes from the service sector, and the workforce is almost completely employed by the service sector. The workforce can no longer be described as an extension of the production line, and to get more philosophical about it, we can extend Herbert Marcuse's argument of the *"one-dimensional man"*.[7]

In his book with the same title, Marcuse made a critical analysis of the effects of society on the modern individual. Although it was written about half a century ago and dealt with a different reality than what we see today, Marcuse is still worth considering. I would add that when driven by the manufacturing mindset, Communist and Capitalist societies tend to focus on treating workers in consideration of their *Competence : Expertise* dimension only (i.e. their labor). In other words, in manufacturing, people are living robots who produce things under measurable conditions.

Although Marcuse provides a part of the argument, the 12-dimensional person I'm talking about is one who understands that managing the 12 dimensions of who you are is how to be your most holistic self, ready to compete across all your interests. Where Marcuse explored the consequences of the one-dimensional man, the agenda here is to propose how to manage the multi-dimensional self of the service leader so that toxic qualities are identified and better removed.

It may not make intuitive sense to apply this approach to our lives – maybe we shouldn't use management tools, systems, concepts and principles to define how we live. To trained businessmen, entrepreneurs, managers and executives, though, this will make sense. The concepts and vocabulary are common and familiar.

Returning to how people are treated in a work setting, factory workers in manufacturing-dominated economies are expected to fulfill roles that are best characterized under what we call the *Competence : Expertise* dimension. Factory managers need only the output from a team's functional abilities so that they do things 'right'. The only result on the line that matters is output – the volume of products deliverable from a person's hands and feet. In a service setting where the server is the service, relying on only the *Competence : Expertise* dimension won't cut it. To get the best from a team, a manager and the managed will do best and be more competitive when they all develop their individual 12 dimensions. It can't be said enough – to be more competitive in service and to both do things right and do the right things, it takes strength in all 12 dimensions.

This evolution has happened throughout the last 50 years, and more intensely over the past two decades. Work moved on from industrial-era manufacturing to the post-industrial Service Age. We need another citizen, worker and server to compete. This is critical on a national level and for those who want to be more competitive than the people who still follow industrial-era manufacturing rules.

There's an increased awareness of Service Science and Service Design. *Amazon.com*, for example, has dozens of books on related topics and the list is growing by the month. Service Science is different in that it focuses on the industrialization of service, and Service Design looks at how services can be created and managed to better lead clients toward specific actions (like buying more products). For a good primer on Service Design, I suggest starting with *This is Service Design Thinking: Basics, Tools, Cases*, by Marc Stickdorn and Jakob Schneider.[8] They tackle the growing field of Service Design and present various articles from leading Service Design specialists. Multidisciplinary and insightful, the book covers many important areas of how to design what I call the Service Habitat.

For example, the article by Kate Blackmon on "Operations Management: The Relentless Quest for Efficiency" is a good presentation of the *industrialization of service*.[8] Blackmon details how McDonald's has deconstructed, analyzed and standardized the service of creating food into a process that consistently hits the financial mark. Sure enough, going to a McDonald's in New York and sitting down for a meal will mostly result in an experience that delivers a very similar look, feel and tastes from a McDonald's in any other city. Whether you're in Los Angeles, Sydney or Paris, the consistency of the experience is what has helped make and keep the company successful.

There are examples of less standardized approaches to service, like the kind we find at large retail companies like Sears or Walmart. These chains are closer to what I'm talking about but they're also not delivering the full, holistic package from their staff.

On this point, I would like to make a special mention of the upscale fashion retailer Nordstrom, which has a renowned approach to training and communicating its service culture. Employees used to get an employee handbook, a small card with the words:

Welcome to Nordstrom

We're glad to have you with our Company. Our number one goal is to provide outstanding customer service. Set both your personal and professional goals high. We have great confidence in your ability to achieve them.

Nordstrom Rules:
Rule #1: Use best judgment in all situations. There will be no additional rules.

Please feel free to ask your department manager, store manager, or division general manager any question at any time.

This has been replaced with the even more concise rule to just use good judgment, along with a handbook of regulations. This fundamental way of doing things shows how a service-oriented company has identified a holistic approach and commitment from its staff.

My mission is to go beyond the *Competence : Expertise* dimension of the service provider to see how to better connect competence, character, and care. Yes, actually caring about others. This approach is much more personal, as it sets the stage for service leadership and lets people understand how a person's functional abilities depend on the harder-to-grasp being side of the service provider.

To use a different analogy, imagine we're biologists in a lab, where the 12 dimensions are different systems that work together to make the body of our personal brand live and breathe. If the 12 dimensions are like the different systems of a body, there's an overarching 'organ' that holds it all together. That organ is conscientiousness, or the blend of mindfulness and persistence. This organ is the commitment to being self-aware and to work on self-improvement. Mindful persistence involves reflecting, being honest to ourselves about what's effective or missing, and continuously trying to improve. From my experience, there's no leader that was born – we all learned how to be leaders through the commitment to being better leaders and better service providers. It is this discipline to improve oneself that will help you grow and develop in each of your dimensions.

To put it another way, mindful persistence is the result of applying a person's "grit" through a filter of reflection. Grit, as Dr. Angela Lee Duckworth explains through her work at the Positive Psychology Center at the University of Pennsylvania, is, "the tendency to sustain interest in and effort toward very long-term goals." Given her research into success, grit is a common quality she's found in all kinds of people who have sustained success. Factors like a person's IQ, EQ, or other similar traits haven't proven as common an ingredient.

Since mindful persistence is what binds the 12 dimensions together, it wouldn't be right to call it a dimension in itself. It could be a personality trait but it's more of a habit you can increasingly use and strengthen. Most successful executives – true service leaders – are conscientious about how they lead and serve their people. There are many variables but the common quality is that they stubbornly work hard at improving themselves, what they do, and how they do it. This is from how they function as leaders within their organization and how they communicate within their companies and the market, to how they present themselves to their own staff, stakeholders, and other people within their working environment.

Again, your conscientiousness is what holds your dimensions together; the 12 dimensions offer a checklist you can use on your own entrepreneurial journey. Like with all journeys, it helps to have a map showing us where to go and what to avoid. To help you understand what each dimension is about and give you a practical approach for improving your own dimensions, each chapter explores the content of the dimension and provides a reminder to move into action. Most importantly, this is a guide you can use to identify your Anna Karenina deficiencies and be a better contributor to the people in your life.

Service is About Contributing to Your Tribe

Strengthening your personal brand can help you address how valuable you are to the people in your life. By continually improving yourself and making yourself more useful to those around you, you benefit materially and psychically, and your feelings of wellbeing and belonging can swell and stay throughout your life.

What this demands from you is mindful persistence, a practice and mindset that holds your 12 dimensions together. This means always learning, and being curious about how to improve the quality of your personal service and who you are. By doing so, you will find that the more you contribute and are trusted as a personal-service leader, the more valued you will be to your tribe and organization. This is what life is all about, or at least is what it is when we are at our best – contributing to our family, friends, community, and ourselves.

I would like to point out that with this kind of information, there's a barrier in the way: inertia. This is when people run on autopilot, a necessary part of life because not to run on autopilot can be exhausting. But this also means it's hard to create new habits and new behaviors built around new ideas. For growth and maturation to occur, it's crucial that new thoughts have the opportunity to become new habits. The ideas around service and the 12 dimensions are meant to result in a change in behavior, and to keep running those behaviors without losing steam after a few days, weeks, months or years. To have a profound impact on your life, you need a way to refresh your motivation and keep acting on the insights you've picked up. This is a key part of the conscientiousness I referred to earlier. If you're trying to create breakthroughs in your life or if you want to spark breakthroughs within your organization, I suggest following the Entrepreneurial Cycle.

The Entrepreneurial Cycle for an Individual

Life is an entrepreneurial journey because we are the entrepreneurs of our lives – no one's ever solved the exact challenges we've had to solve, and dealt with the people we've crossed paths with in our lives. The Entrepreneurial Cycle on the individual level is the first step you can use to explore the 12 dimensions of your personal brand. After you apply this for yourself and get your own house in order, you can then apply it to your organization. The Entrepreneurial Cycle for the individual is in Figure 3, below.

ACTION!

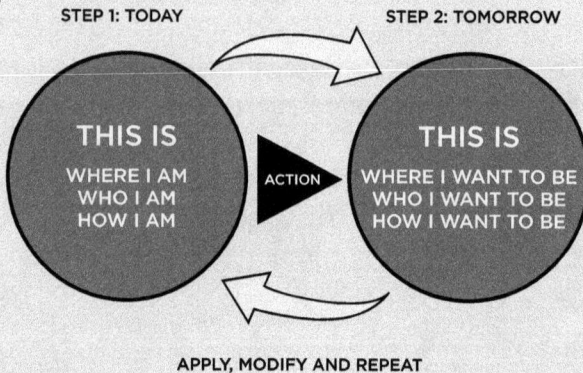

Figure 3: The Entrepreneurial Cycle for an Individual

The Entrepreneurial Cycle is a skill that everyone should know. It's easy and all it takes is the dedication to sit down and do it. The process has four parts:

Step 1: TODAY
Get a clear sense of your present situation. Write down where you live, work, have fun and the different environments you are in. You also need to describe who you are. This includes the people and things that are important to you, what you're good at, what excites you and makes you tick, as

well as the behaviors and personal qualities that you would like to change.

Step 2: TOMORROW
Make an inventory of what you would like to be in the future. Although *Tomorrow* can literally mean tomorrow, it can also mean one or five years from now.

Step 3: ACTION
Decide what you need to do to move from *Today* to *Tomorrow*. Define and carry out all actions, great and small, to help move toward your goal.

Step 4: APPLY, MODIFY AND REPEAT
This is a tool you can use for the rest of your life. It's a powerful way of applying a strategic review process to planning where you will put your energy.

The Entrepreneurial Cycle for an Organization
The Entrepreneurial Cycle is also useful for bringing about change and growth in an organization. It is similar to the model for an individual, with a few small adaptations. The second version of the Entrepreneurial Cycle is illustrated in Figure 4, below.

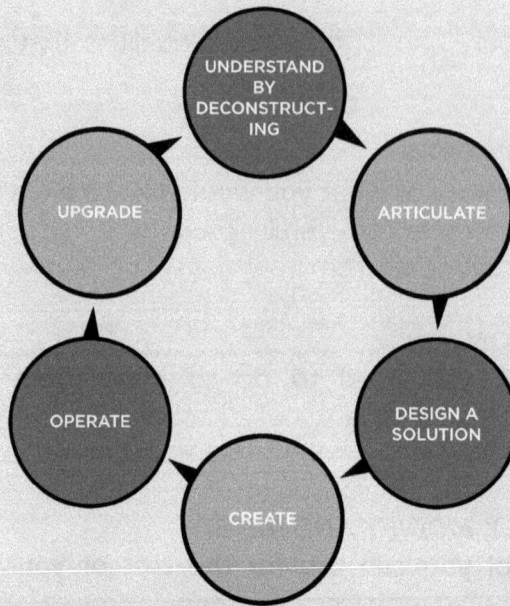

Figure 4: The Entrepreneurial Cycle for an Organization

The steps of the Entrepreneurial Cycle for the organization are:

1. Understand by Deconstructing – Once you've identified an area that needs to be upgraded, deconstruct it as much as you can to identify the different variables and elements that affect one another. Look at the people, situation, pressures, resources, and environmental conditions that created the problem.

2. Articulate – The entrepreneurial process is about creating a solution that resonates with others. By articulating the problem after identifying its various parts, you are beginning to structure a path to your solution. This also helps focus your team's intelligence and experience around the problem.

3. Design a Solution – With your associates, design a specific application that addresses the problem. Remember that the solution should address the elements identified in deconstruction from Step 1.

4. Create – Build your 'prototype' – the result of your design process.

5. Operate – With prototype in hand – be it an actual device, process, or organization of resources – operate it to see if it solves the problem.

6. Upgrade – Review the results of operating your solution to see if it satisfies all the issues that created your problem in the first place. If needed, run the Cycle again to get a stronger solution that works.

A major hurdle in the application of the 12 dimensions is to understand how each one fits from within the context of your own life. For this reason, the Entrepreneurial Cycle for the Individual is probably the best first plan of action. Then, you can bring together your tribe to help design and apply a solution that helps break through your challenges – the Entrepreneurial Cycle for the Organization.

Each chapter includes a case study

Using a central character called Sharon, a restaurant owner and chef at a successful French restaurant called *Le Petit Plat*, these hypothetical situations illustrate how each dimension can play a significant, if not deciding factor in a person's business and life. Although this uses the example of a small business owner in the Food & Beverage sector – from an obviously recognizable service company, the idea is to demonstrate how the 12 dimensions are relevant. In this case, as the word *chef* comes from the French word for leader, this is as good an example as any for showing how service leadership comes through personal service. In a restaurant, the food on the plates and the greater business are the outcomes of the dimensions working together. The success that a restaurant, its habitat, staff and customers are able to achieve starts with the 12 dimensions of the chef's personal brand. We have also decided to use one central story, instead of a collection of different cases, in order to keep things more focused. Having 12 different people or companies could have distracted from the chapter's topic.

A Future Built by Competitive Service Leaders

If life really is an entrepreneurial journey, then this stage in my own journey has been dedicated to mapping the territory of the service leader. I have explored and exercised the practice of service leadership and I hope the observations and lessons I've picked up along the way will help you as well.

We live in an era of change and unprecedented technological development. Those among us who remember a time when there were no computers in an office or classroom, let alone your pocket, can attest to the phenomenal growth that has come with the innovations of our age. The Internet has so deeply woven itself into our lives that it is where technology powerfully influences our social and personal lives. This evolution has added new conditions to how people relate to one another and our cultures are quickly adapting and evolving. It is a truly wondrous time to be alive, with tremendous possibilities and potential still waiting to be discovered and realized.

It's also true that the more things change, the more they remain the same. After the far-reaching power of the manufacturing mindset and its revolutions, we now find ourselves back again in service. It's been there all along, only now we need to get back to the principles and practices of service leadership if we are to reach our greatest aspirations. This isn't about making, selling and getting more stuff; it's about living and experiencing greater, more fulfilled lives. When done, I hope you will also understand and align your own life to be a better service provider and even come out as a service leader.

If remembering all 12 dimensions seems daunting, bear in mind that these dimensions are what we get after trying to separate the main dimensions of the service leader. To be complete, it should be at least 12, even if they are hard to remember. Collectively they will help you strengthen what I call the 3-Cs of your service potential.

The 3-Cs are your Competence, Character and Care

A healthy balance of all three is the hallmark of a true service leader. The 3-Cs will be explained in greater detail in the next chapter. For now, let's start by asserting that the worth of a service leader is measured by the degree to which he or she acts with Competence, Character and Care.

To put it graphically, under the rules of the Service Age, one's leadership potential is where the 3-Cs overlap (Figure 5).

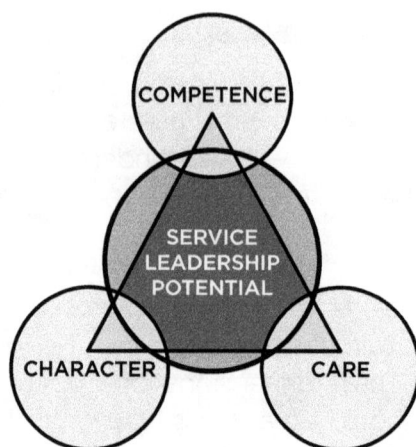

Figure 5: The 3-Cs and Service Leadership Potential

Competence, Character and Care is the shorthand, and the full 12 dimensions are the checklist to cover all aspects of who you are as a service leader. Moreover, this checklist can help you identify if you have a quality within you that will trigger the Anna Karenina Principle, ultimately dooming your leadership efforts to failure.

The 3-Cs of Service Leadership

As described in the previous section, the key ingredients behind a great service leader can be summed up as the person's 3-Cs of Competence, Character and Care. By making each one as strong as possible, the intersection of the 3-Cs is our leadership potential. This is also the building block for establishing and maintaining our level of trustworthiness.

Competence is that we know what to do through your *Competence : Expertise* dimension. Character feeds into it, especially for building trust, which will be covered in Chapter 5, on your *Moral : Character* dimension. This is important, because it highlights that even if we can get a job done, things will fall apart if our people question our character. This will manifest as anxiety about our motives, most likely resulting in weakening engagement from our people who may even flat-out refuse to cooperate. The third C is Care, because it's critical that a leader expresses authentic concern for everyone involved with the team, either within the group or those beyond it. In other words, leaders achieve greatness as a measure of how deeply they care and are not selfish – they care about the team, the group's collective success, and even how stakeholders and clients feel about the products and services they may be receiving.

We can use this approach to review political movements. For example, Communism is effective at delivering on the functional needs and capacities of a society, as we're seeing in today's Communist nations. Where Communism falls short is around supporting the character and care of the population. Within the Communist system, people are no less motivated by self-interest than in Capitalism but they aren't as driven by selfless care. They surely care about their survival and the ability to feed the population (although even this isn't necessarily true when, for example, we look at North Korea), but the care needed to uphold the rights of the individual is much weaker. We now have decades of Communism in practice and we see that in execution and delivery, the system isn't as utopic as imagined. That's why countries around the world may acknowledge the Communist countries' hard power but aren't inspired to adopt Communism at home.

Care is expressed as compassion, not being selfish and having empathy for others. The degree to which a service provider communicates care is what wins loyalty. On a professional level, care can help drive a team toward excellence when no other reason may be there. People with great levels of care are passionate about what they are doing, expressed as a commitment to the organization's mission as extended to the group.

For a good example of a business leader who displays strong competence on all three, we can look at the legendary value investor, Warren Buffett, from Berkshire Hathaway Inc. Through his actions and writing, we can see that he is strong on all three. Equally legendary is Microsoft founder Bill Gates, who has also proven to be well rounded. In politics, if we look at former US president Bill Clinton, we see that he is exceptionally competent, and his ability to deliver beyond competence is what has built his enduring appeal.

Since these are not absolutes – you can have relatively more or less of any of them – many have one or two that are strong out of the three. When this happens, things can go badly. Some people have had extremely strong functional Competence and Character qualities but lack Care – extreme examples include Adolf Hitler, Joseph Stalin and Pol Pot. These men were extremely strong in the skills of ruling over others but were utterly missing or toxic in their Care.

The 3-Cs of a service leader is the easy-to-remember model for keeping our eye on the value and path to great service leadership. Much as this is a useful tool for daily management or reflection, it's not enough if the goal is to make a deeper 'detox' of our service leadership. For that, we have the 12 dimensions, described in the following chapters. As we move forward and review each dimension, I invite you to keep an open mind and light heart. Bravely face all aspects of what makes you *you*, and remember that the benefit of this honest exploration is that you will end up being a far more effective – *competitive* – service leader. You can anticipate feeling better about who you are, because after this kind of detox who you are will actually be better.

May this part of your entrepreneurial journey be as rewarding as it is revealing!

The *Competence : Expertise* Dimension

Chapter Summary:
This dimension involves all the abilities, competencies, and talents needed to succeed across operational duties and what would be listed in a job description.

In order to produce better work and be a more competitive service leader, take stock of your competencies with a realistic appreciation of the skills you have. Together, these are the ingredients in your *Competence : Expertise* dimension. By strengthening and broadening this dimension, you can better make a living or contribute to your various tribes and social groups. This is true for your career, volunteer work or any other activity that demands the ability to complete a formal task. The *Competence : Expertise* dimension is what normally gets noticed first – this is typically what employers ask about when you're looking for work. Job descriptions are mostly structured around functions that a competent person in that role would carry out, and although critical, it would be a mistake to think this alone guarantees success – especially in service.

Put another way, when people turn to us for our expertise, the unsaid expectation from them could be what can we do to either help or advance their goals? There could also be a hidden motive that these people can get something from us that will give them an advantage.

To see what this might look like in practice, consider the act of visiting a doctor for an annual check-up. The reason we pick one doctor over the others is mostly due to how convenient the access will be and our trust in the care we expect to receive. The first concern is logistical, and the most important factor is whether that doctor will or won't deliver the level of functional competence we need and expect. This dimension is especially important when considering present needs – what's in it for us, right now. On the other hand, the service provider and leader who can go beyond the immediate situation to fulfill the other dimensions is the one who will have a more developed personal brand. This person has a better chance of winning our loyalty.

This dimension should and does dominate attention, but the higher up you go in a group, the less you need skills that are technical in nature. The more you deal with operating or producing things, the more you need to do things right; the more you deal with making decisions and leading, the greater the need to do the right things. This is tied to the fact that doing things right is about delivering excellence in production, whereas doing the right things is about delivering excellence in service.

In principle, the overarching quality of a healthy *Competence : Expertise* dimension is that you have cognitive competence. In other words, that your mind is itself healthy and whole enough to exercise competence and expertise in thought and action. This is more specifically covered in the *Mental : Intellectual* dimension later on. But for now it's enough to say that for your competence or expertise to shine through, it has to be assumed that a person has a minimum cognitive ability to do things. If not, failure might be the only result.

To get more specific, two skills from this dimension that everyone would benefit from strengthening are strategic planning and communication. As described earlier in the Entrepreneurial Cycle, defining a vision and setting steps to reach that goal is an important skill that crosses sectors and disciplines. It's amazing that this isn't taught in high school or earlier. It's essential because as the entrepreneurs of our lives we must develop ourselves to provide best service to the people we cross paths with. Not taking the time to see where we are and to better aim at what and where we would like to be is like putting life on autopilot and just coasting. It's possible that success might be in the future, but the chances of success are much higher when there is a consistent target with a plan for how to get there.

By completing the Entrepreneurial Cycle that we've included throughout this book, you will apply a tool that can deliver an explicit list of things for you to do. This list isn't only of academic importance – it's also of strategic importance. It helps you aim better for the targets you've chosen. In case the list of things to do is long and daunting, remember that sometimes it's best to pick out the items that are most important or make the most strategic sense. Get these out of the way and the rest should fall into place.

Another essential tool in your *Competence : Expertise* dimension is your functional ability to communicate thoughts and ideas, either in writing or through speech. No matter who you are or what you do, improving the quality of your communication is a great way to enhance your competitive edge. For example, when several candidates compete for the same role and they all have equivalent functional abilities, the standard people often use to judge between candidates is communication skills (even if it's unconscious).

Imagine we have three managers in a district and each one is great at running their office. When the time comes to reward or promote the one who brings added value, the decision usually favors the one who writes better reports, delivers stronger presentations, or has better networking skills.

On the whole, most of what schools and professional education focus on is our *Competence : Expertise* dimension. As mentioned earlier, although we must develop functional abilities to get anything done, there is much more to service leadership and who we are that has not been addressed. Some schools and Liberal Arts programs are beginning to weave in training around our other dimensions, but these aren't as common as they need to be. In the Service Age, a multidimensional approach should be universal.

At its most basic, a pure focus on the *Competence : Expertise* dimension is a "one-dimensional man". This has traditionally been enough to fill roles often seen on a production line, since manufacturing companies pay for labor that delivers primarily or exclusively on this dimension. In fact, it's common to see a production line with people who speak different languages but who can still fulfill their quota.

The *Competence : Expertise* dimension contains what we do, especially when others pay for our effort. In a work setting, this is the value we contribute to help our organization run smoothly and efficiently, including but not limited to: technical abilities, literacy, computer skills, math skills, and exercising various levels of professional expertise. This dimension also includes how we delegate and project-manage, run operational tasks, and other high-level behaviors.

Since we're looking at this from the filter of branding, it helps to also consider the ways that product branding can extend to personal brand building. For products, the *Competence : Expertise* dimension includes qualities such as whether food tastes good and fills our stomach, whether a beverage tastes good and quenches our thirst, or how well the clothes cover and protect our bodies from injury or the elements. This dimension is straightforward. How we expand this dimension is by going to school, reading books and even mimicking people we admire or respect. We can improve this dimension by getting a deeper understanding of how things work and what we can do across different situations.

Let's say your job is to fix jet engines; your functional abilities will improve if you actively try to get more training, and your performance will improve if you take the time to better understand the theoretical basis of how jets work. Although theoretical knowledge doesn't suit everyone, there's no question that a deeper understanding can translate into more effective operational abilities. This point is also true when delivering service.

In the best-selling book, *Zen and the Art of Motorcycle Maintenance: An Inquiry into Values*, Robert Pirsig presented two mental models for understanding what happens through experience.[9] He called these the Romantic or Classical models. The Romantic is the Zen approach, which focuses on what is happening at any given moment. The other is the Classical model, which aims to understand the inner workings of things and to master the mechanics behind how things work.

To illustrate the point, imagine flipping a light switch. The Romantic model accepts that flipping the switch is what makes light appear, in and of itself. For the Classical mind, flipping the switch is an action that closes an electrical circuit that allows an electrical current to pass through a fluorescent tube that emits light of a certain wavelength when a current passes across two electrodes under a vacuum. Anyone looking to develop their Competence : Expertise dimension would benefit from applying the Classical approach to how they themselves work and get things done. This lets them rationally break down their competencies into separate parts and find which skills are missing or may need to be improved.

The Classical model is a good approach if you want to identify the internal switches that help you improve how you get things done in an operational sense. A clear appreciation of your *Competence : Expertise* dimension can help you identify functional gaps that need to be filled, and it will also show if anything is missing or defective, as well as where your other dimensions affect the quality of your service.

Let's imagine we're picking a lawyer to help us on a case. For many service providers like lawyers, there's a basic assumption that the person we're about to hire has a minimum functional competence. Often, we hope the person can deliver a service that is even higher than our needs, an added value when the professional can go beyond what it takes to get the job done. A lawyer who fails to measure up to our expectations will quickly get a bad review and, over time, a bad reputation. If the level is especially low – mostly based on our expectation of what we think a basic standard should be – we might even make a big stink about this person's incompetence.

Although it can be hard to clearly list the positive characteristics we expect in others or ourselves, it's easier to state the negative qualities we must avoid. For example, we may not consciously acknowledge or reward a lawyer for being an especially good writer, but we would probably be not best pleased if we discovered this lawyer couldn't effectively write about our side of the case. Similarly, although it's not a reflex for everyone to praise or acknowledge how hard someone has worked on a project, many managers are quick to reprimand laziness or the kind of functional incompetence that sticks out like a sore thumb.

In *What Management Is: How It Works and Why It's Everyone's Business*, Joan Magretta and Nan Stone explain that in order to manage effectively you have to first understand what works.[10] In our *Competence : Expertise* dimension, by making an inventory of who we are and what works, we can start to address what's missing. We can enrol in training to upgrade our functional or technical skills as needed. From a managerial perspective, if there are people in our group who are missing important skills, we can help train them. This can be accomplished through your human resources department, enrolling people in formal training, mentoring, or by any number of other training approaches. It's worth noting that when it comes to leading or managing in a work setting, what's often missing is the mindful persistence I referred to earlier. Most people simply don't have the grit or discipline to keep hammering away, or to dig deep enough and follow through in their pursuits toward self or team improvement. However, if you aim for leadership with a goal to be the most beneficial manager for your team, it is crucial to have that mindful persistence.

Anyone interested in deeper insights on this topic should refer to *The Leadership Challenge: How to Make Extraordinary Things Happen in Organizations*, by Kouzes and Posner.[2] The pair have produced renowned material on the subject of leadership, and, in their view, true leadership has less to do with personality and much more to do with behavior. They surveyed thousands in order to sharpen what people mean when they refer to a signature leadership experience. They found common themes and practices, such as leaders, "model the way, inspire a shared vision, challenge the process, enable others to act, and encourage the heart." Books like this one can be a great source of inspiration and guidance around your *Competence : Expertise* dimension.

To be a better manager and gain specific insights on how to

upgrade the *Competence : Expertise* dimension, a great place to start is taking courses offered in most MBA programs. MBA schools mainly focus on improving the functional abilities of budding managers, with classes on topics including strategic planning, accounting, finance, marketing, and statistical analysis. These are all valid skills managers must have to get ahead.

This dimension is critical, but a growing number of companies are finding that hiring only on competence is a losing strategy.

As a troublesome observation, I note that a large percentage of current corporate leaders are trained accountants or lawyers. This accountant-led or lawyer-led leadership is the default position for many companies when the economic climate is tough and belt-tightening and restructuring are what's needed to stay afloat. It's a survival tactic that often puts innovative energy and forward thinking in the back seat. Over the past few years, the economic climate certainly has challenged many companies, so accountant-led leadership has made sense for many firms. Also, when the economic climate demands that companies take more defensive positions because of legal pressures, the executive suite typically gets populated with lawyers. For many companies, depending on the needs, we see three main archetypes in the executive suite: the entrepreneurial director, the accountant and the lawyer.

When companies get beyond a certain size and begin to lose their competitive edge, the accountant-led leadership can seem the best path for survival. The issue with this is that there isn't a strong creative vision or voice to keep asking what comes next. After all, the accounting discipline is a practice of looking back at what has been done, or what the performance was. The accounting mindset and operational skills are not focused on innovation or inspiration.

If we take today's DHL, the growth model is still being driven by the culture we built while I was there. However, there is the danger that a functional-only mindset will take over, which can raise issues in a service context. DHL began and was built around the insistence of decentralization, so a centralized model might lead to lower performance and decreased competitiveness. When we're dealing with a large corporation like DHL, certain areas must be centralized in order to maintain quality of service. Budgeting has to be centralized, or else everything turns into a big mess. Operationally, however, large service-oriented companies can't be centralized. I don't believe centralized leadership is the optimal model for a service provider. For DHL, each city has to manage itself. If not, what you get is industrialization of the service delivery process, which addresses the functional needs but isn't going to result in a strong, problem-solving service culture that maintains its competitive edge.

McDonald's, the most familiar example of the industrialization of service, has fast-food as the commodity and the service is tightly defined. This has been profoundly successful for McDonald's, as their brand is about replicating the core service across different branches. However, although this works on the *Competence : Expertise* dimension, this service delivery mostly works because it doesn't demand problem-solvers around customer-needs. Any room for improvisation is limited to as close to zero as possible. This isn't the path to great service leadership (and makes for a poor model for personal excellence).

To end this discussion on the *Competence : Expertise* dimension, I will stress the Anna Karenina Principle and how it relates to your own life. You must watch out for qualities in your dimension that may corrupt the strength of this dimension and how it may spill over to your other dimensions. For example, if you are competent but have a tendency to shout or be belligerent when stressed, or speak with discriminatory language, this could be the element that eventually brings you to service failure. This small defect that you might brush off as unimportant for whatever reason, could be the reason that you fail to attract followers or repel the ones you do have – two things you never want to experience when you're a service leader.

When exploring this dimension, it will only be complete if you diligently and conscientiously try to find what in your dimension is toxic and take active steps to weed out your particular shortcomings.

ACTION!

STEP 1: TODAY   **STEP 2: TOMORROW**

THIS IS

WHERE I AM
WHO I AM
HOW I AM

ACTION

THIS IS

WHERE I WANT TO BE
WHO I WANT TO BE
HOW I WANT TO BE

APPLY, MODIFY AND REPEAT

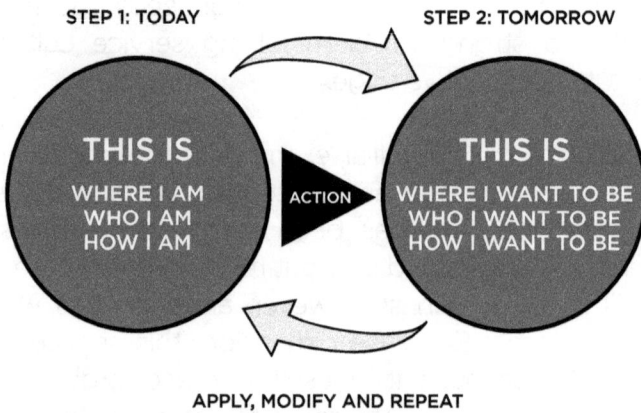

If you feel your *Competence : Expertise* dimension needs strengthening, it helps if you can make a deeper, more precise review of what specifically is missing. For example, let's say that you recognize that your presentation skills need to be upgraded. Explore where your discomfort comes from, or why limiting thoughts are inhibiting your behavior.

Step 1: TODAY
Get a clear sense of your present situation. Write down the

elements of your *Competence : Expertise* dimension that affect where and how you live, work, and have fun in the different environments of your day-to-day world.

1. _____

2. _____

3. _____

4. _____

5. _____

Step 2: TOMORROW
Make an inventory of what you would like to be in the future. Although *Tomorrow* can literally mean tomorrow, it can also mean one or five years from now.

1. _____

2. _____

3. _____

4. _____

5. _____

Step 3: ACTION
Decide what you need to do to move from *Today* to *Tomorrow*. Define and carry out all actions, great and small, to help move toward your goal.

1. _____

2. _____

3. _____

4. _____

5. _____

Step 4: APPLY, MODIFY, AND REPEAT

TOP CHEF IN ACTION – THE *COMPETENCE : EXPERTISE* DIMENSION

Sharon's been running her French restaurant *Le Petit Plat* for two years and things are going well. Now she wants to completely change the menu. A recent review in a leading food and wine magazine could have been better, so Sharon wants to make a broad refresh of the main courses and appetizers.

Sharon's *Competence : Expertise* dimension includes her skills at creating new dishes that are consistent with fine French cooking, but will also surprise diners with their novelty, quality and finesse. Sharon prides herself on designing new dishes that showcase her expertise, but she also knows she must create dishes that her staff can reproduce and deliver.

Sharon's *Competence : Expertise* dimension also includes her abilities with classic French ingredients, cooking methods, how to design an appealing menu that her team can maintain, how to ensure the ambiance at *Le Petit Plat* is appropriate to attract her desired clientele, and how to run the business so that the margins on each plate are enough to ensure a healthy profit.

The *Moral : Character* Dimension

Chapter Summary:
This dimension is arguably the most important element of your personal brand – falter on this dimension and you can quickly lose your moral authority, respect and then your followers. The key is to behave in ways that are consistent with high values like those listed in the British Association for Counselling and Psychotherapy (BACP), and rid yourself of the viruses that can corrupt your moral authority.

The next dimension we will look at is also the most important one when it comes to service leadership. Your *Moral : Character* dimension holds the qualities about you that can't be seen, but inform what you do and how others see you. Just as how you see morals or the lack of them in others, and sometimes judge people because of it, other people do it with you based on how they interpret your behavior.

Your morals are the subjective values picked up from parents, throughout childhood, and refined with experience. Like your physical health, when morals are sound they will probably go unnoticed, but when they're bad they can have a profound negative impact. With bad morals, it's hard to define where the lines are, but everyone has their own red lines that can't or shouldn't be crossed.

One way to review this dimension is by returning to the mind-as-computer analogy we described in the section on the POS, or Personal Operating System. If your mind is a computer, your morals are the algorithms that set actions as right or wrong, ethical or unethical. Traditionally, moral directives were taught by religious customs. For example, the Old Testament defines a moral code through the Ten Commandments and associated teachings, and this was succeeded by Christianity's additions and moral distinctions. I have found that moral directives from across the spectrum of religious faiths run roughly parallel to each other. Although they are not the same from one tradition to the other, there are some common fundamentals across the many faiths.

For example, each tradition has a variant of the Golden Rule, which advises to do unto others as you would have done unto you. The reverse, sometimes called the Silver Rule, advises you to avoid behaviors that you wouldn't want done unto you. This 'negative' of the Golden Rule is more common to Confucianism and the Asian mindset. The point is that many traditions address the *Moral : Character* dimension and they all cover similar ground.

For a more contemporary set of conduct guidelines, there are Benjamin Franklin's 13 virtues, or we can use the even more current qualities defined by the British Association for Counselling and Psychotherapy (BACP). Whether it's Confucius, Franklin, or the BACP, the details may vary but the ingredients seem to be universally valid. Here is the BACP's list:

Empathy: the ability to communicate understanding of another person's experience from that person's perspective.

Sincerity: a personal commitment to consistency between what is professed and what is done.

Integrity: commitment to being moral in dealings with others, personal straightforwardness, honesty and coherence.

Resilience: the capacity to work with the client's concerns without being personally diminished.

Respect: showing appropriate esteem to others and their understanding of themselves.

Humility: the ability to assess accurately and acknowledge one's own strengths and weaknesses.

Competence: the effective deployment of the skills and knowledge needed to do what is required.

Fairness: the consistent application of appropriate criteria to inform decisions and actions.

Wisdom: possession of sound judgment that informs practice.

Courage: the capacity to act in spite of known fears, risks and uncertainty.

For anyone making a review of their *Moral : Character* dimension, contrasting their morals against this list could strengthen their moral authority and ability to stay true when the going gets tough. It's interesting to note that the notion of sin is missing from the list. With sin, you're either in need of some kind of redemption or you must always work to remain free of sinful behavior. The concept of sin is also missing from the traditional Chinese moral canon, where the roots of the nation's moral past are in Confucianism. I have argued that it is unfortunate that the Communist Revolution brought an explicit if not violent rejection of the country's moral foundation, and now we're finding a country whose service leaders seem to lack the critical moral compass and moral authority to lead in the right direction.

In my classes, I've found it challenging to explain what to do in order to be a moral person. Advising students to stay honest didn't have the sticking power I was looking for. Then, when I flipped it around so that I was telling students to avoid the opposite, it had the impact I was looking for. Rather than saying service leaders must stay honest, it is more 'real' to say, just don't be dishonest. To put it another way, rather than trying to always tell the truth, I advise that true service leaders do not lie.

Being moral or not matters and often surfaces when facing a difficult situation. The conditions of your life will hand you many situations where you can behave morally or not. So, when talking to our friends, we must remember to be fair and trustworthy and not to be too concerned about self correction and shame. Or, it's like telling someone to be polite, which can mean many things to different people. What's more practical is to flip it around and say, just don't be rude. The notion of politeness is vague, but we all understand what being rude is. Parents who tell their kids to behave and be good are giving less practical advice than saying, just don't be bad. We all learn early on what bad behavior is, so my advice to kids is simply *don't be bad* and then I let them take it from there. As a guide for my students, I offer the classic Confucian list of virtues, adapted as their negative so that they know what to avoid (Figure 6, below).

CONFUCIAN VIRTUES	ADAPTED (CONFUCIAN NEGATIVE)
仁:KINDNESS	DON'T BE UNKIND
義:RIGHTEOUSNESS	DON'T BE UNFAIR
禮:RESPECT	DON'T BE RUDE
智:WISDOM	DON'T BE FOOLISH
信:TRUSTWORTHINESS	DON'T BE UNTRUSTWORTHY
忠:LOYALTY	DON'T BE DISLOYAL
勇:COURAGE	DON'T BE COWARDLY
廉:UNCORRUPTED	DON'T BE CORRUPTIBLE
恥:SHAME	DON'T BE SHAMELESS
孝:CARE FOR THE OLD	DON'T ABUSE THE OLD
悌:CARE FOR THE YOUNG	DON'T ABUSE THE YOUNG
改:SELF-CORRECTION	DON'T REFUSE TO CORRECT WHEN YOU ARE WRONG
恕:FORGIVENESS	DON'T HOLD A GRUDGE

Figure 6. The Confucian Virtues and their Opposites

When auditing your *Moral : Character* dimension, remember that all traditions have merits, sometimes overlapping with each one addressing its own moral landscape and code of conduct. Some aspects of one may not be included in another, but, even if you only stick to one tradition, it should do.

If success, personal development and growth are your goals, there is great value in reviewing each tradition and taking what makes sense from each. See what's common or unique and apply the best and most useful to your own life and situation.

Even if you don't feel a need to choose a particular tradition, following the laws and mores set by civil society will also work. Nearly all of us were brought up under the values from our parents, and we can benefit from these traditions. If you want to enhance your personal brand to be the best it can be, choose wisely from what was given to you and what you can learn from other traditions. Then, when the time comes, you can pass your special moral code on to your children, your peers, your team, and beyond.

I believe we've internalized our tribe's core values by the time we're five or six years old. These core values are mostly set at a young age, with later development coming through reflection on our experience. This is probably because we're members within our tribes and to maintain the strength and health of the group, we isolate those who fail to follow the tribe's codes. Individually, we must manage our behavior so that we aren't left out in the cold if our tribe goes through major change. By refining this dimension, we're not only clarifying our usefulness to our tribe but we're also making ourselves more competitive.

With service being such an important facet of human society and civilization, we can now see why contributing to our groups and helping our families, friends, and associates succeed is the path to the greatest fulfillment.

As children, we can take and use resources without worrying about giving back. Once we reach a certain age or ability, we're expected to do our fair share and begin to contribute. If we keep taking and fail to give back we get reprimanded, corrected and maybe even shunned. Our societies are also built to recognize that beyond a certain age, if we can't contribute as much, or at all, as a group we should care for those who are unable to care for themselves. Therefore, if during our years when we are able to pitch in we failed to do so, on some level we may feel the sting of rebuke or rejection when our time of need arrives.

On the economic side, one criticism of capitalism is that over the long term, the mission to generate profit invariably leads to behavior that is destructive and immoral. As I see it, profitmaking isn't moral or immoral, but is *amoral*; that is, lacking any moral content or value. That being said, the *Moral : Character* dimension of corporate leadership sets the moral direction and climate within a company. When we see a company whose operations seem not to be guided by a stable, inspiring moral compass, what we see is the absence of strong *Moral : Character* dimensions from the people at the top.

For example, a large bank based in Hong Kong was censured for its role in laundering funds from terrorist and drug organizations. The bank laundered more than US$880 million for international drug cartels, and channeled about US$660 million for banks listed in US-sanctioned countries. As of this writing, the bank was fined and it lost some of its business.

That the bank did this was not a failure because of the company's moral code. As an amoral entity, the bank is simply the vehicle people with corrupted *Moral : Character* dimensions were using to make their financial transactions. The failure was in the *Moral : Character* dimension of its leadership. Feeding into this is the mistaken idea that we can expect businesses to have different values and moral codes; that there are your values in your home and your values at the office. This is false. The fundamental morality of a company is set by senior management – they set the standard, defend and personify what is and isn't acceptable. So when the bank's staff put profit above moral justice and didn't exercise sound, moral judgment, this moral failure was a reflection of the values and morals held by senior management.

It's disheartening to find that when I need an example of a large corporation whose leadership has failed due to a corrupted *Moral : Character* dimension, I can always find a fresh case from banking or finance. The banks have, admittedly, been demonized, but there's no question that they don't deserve it.

The conflict of interest between profit making and maintaining moral authority comes from decision-making that only looks at the short-term. Toxic behavior can easily slip by at the beginning, but over the long run, companies that have less moral authority inevitably fall apart due to the toxic load they keep accumulating.

For example, if we consider a large US-based investment banking group, it looks like the company lost its moral compass after it went public. Here is an incredibly strong company with a long history, but going public seems to have triggered a suppression of their *Moral : Character* dimension. What we have now is a company led by people with incredibly strong *Competence : Expertise* dimensions, but weak, if not outright toxic, *Moral : Character* dimensions. This is likely because when the company was private and the partners were ultimately responsible, there was the inner guidance and moral compass set by the partners. However, now that the company is led by corporate executives, when things go wrong they get fired and leave under a lucrative, golden parachute, only to be replaced with the next round of executives.

For the budding entrepreneur, small-company business leader, manager and director, remember that you must actively manage your *Moral : Character* dimension if you want a strong and healthy team. When you're small, all your people can't help but watch and follow your lead. You have to walk the straight and narrow because your critical pool – your suppliers, customers, staff and everyone else – is watching you for an idea of where everyone is headed.

Remember that when everything is going well, you and others won't notice the content and character of this dimension. It's especially true when what you say fits what the people around you already believe. Once you lose your moral authority, people will stop following you, serving with you or even cooperating with you.

ACTION!

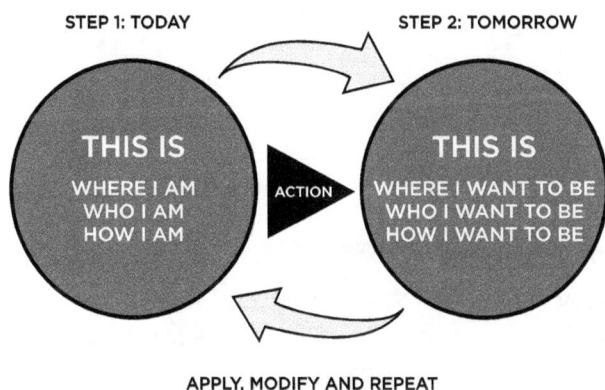

STEP 1: TODAY   STEP 2: TOMORROW

THIS IS
WHERE I AM
WHO I AM
HOW I AM

ACTION

THIS IS
WHERE I WANT TO BE
WHO I WANT TO BE
HOW I WANT TO BE

APPLY, MODIFY AND REPEAT

Review your *Moral : Character* dimension and decide if it needs strengthening. Making a review can be difficult because it's hard to measure our own moral strength against a golden ideal. One reliable approach is to take any of the classical moral guidelines – either from Benjamin Franklin or the British Association for Counselling and Psychotherapy (BACP) set listed above, or any other – and see if you behaved well and in accordance with them. Again, if reviewing your behavior is too vague, think about the opposite as a guide for what to simply not do. For example, if being respectful is too hard to fairly assess, avoid being disrespectful instead. If there have been instances where your disrespect has acted against your best interests, and this was a toxic quality in your behavior and personal service, then you now know what to work on.

Step 1: TODAY

Get a clear sense of your present situation. Write down the elements of your *Moral : Character* dimension that affect where and how you live, work, and have fun in the different environments of your day-to-day world.

1. _____

2. _____

3. _____

4. _____

5. _____

Step 2: TOMORROW

Make an inventory of what you would like to be in the future. Although *Tomorrow* can literally mean tomorrow, it can also mean one or five years from now.

1. _____

2. _____

3. _____

4. _____

5. _____

Step 3: ACTION

Decide what you need to do to move from *Today* to *Tomorrow*. Define and carry out all actions great and small to help move toward your goal.

1. _____

2. _____

3. _____

4. _____

5. _____

Step 4: APPLY, MODIFY, AND REPEAT

TOP CHEF IN ACTION - THE *MORAL : CHARACTER* DIMENSION

When Sharon began working in the restaurant business, she started as a lowly line cook in a little café. The manager at the time would often lose his temper whenever the pressure was on, treat junior staff badly, and be so rude and disrespectful that sometimes staff would quit. At *Le Petit Plat*, Sharon envisioned a different approach.

Sharon's *Moral : Character* dimension was more informed by what she didn't want to be than by what she thought she should be. She was so turned off by her experience with the impatient, rude and offensive café manager that she decided she would never be that way, no matter what. She appreciated that as the business owner and boss, it was her duty to make the tough decisions - that depending on how she handled herself, she would either win over employees or lose them due to bad morale and loss of respect. No matter how hectic it was in the kitchen, no matter how much noise or conflict the other staff would bring to work, Sharon understood that the mood in the kitchen was set by her example.

She always tried not be unfair, hear each employee out when the time was right, never be rude or dismissive, and be the kind of leader who inspired the best in her team. However, when discipline or corrections were needed, mostly in order to maintain *Le Petit Plat*'s reputation as one of the finest restaurants around, Sharon was firm, stubborn, and decisive.

These qualities were hard to maintain, especially in times of conflict, but the ultimate benefit to the team was that all her staff understood her behavior, and they repaid her with trust and loyalty.

Chapter
SIX

The *Care : Compassion* Dimension

> **Chapter Summary:**
> This dimension is about raising the level of empathy you have for others and not being selfish – your clients, colleagues, friends and family – in order to connect with their deeper needs and help them fulfill those needs.

When thinking about this dimension, I'm reminded of former US president Theodore Roosevelt, who said, "Nobody cares how much you know, until they know how much you care." When thinking about your *Care : Compassion* dimension, remember that this dimension is probably why you, your peers, or the people you admire go the extra mile. This notion of the extra mile is hard to define and hard to expect – imagine a job that tried to quantify a bonus around each time you went the extra mile on a project. On the other hand, when people truly care and behave in ways that show they care, that is highly valued.

This is such an important dimension for service leadership that it's the third C in the 3-Cs described above. Again, the shorthand of the 12 dimensions is expressed as one's Competence, Character and Care.

The roots of caring and compassion are in empathy, and we could even argue that human civilization is the result of how groups organize and formalize the acts of caring. For example, putting food aside for later or for those who might need it is an act of empathy that ensures survival of the group, both in survival terms and also in terms of social harmony. We find that people grossly lacking in this dimension are narcissists and sociopaths who can threaten the survival of the group itself. There have been some recent articles claiming a link between leaders of some organizations and their level of narcissism and lack of empathy. Although such leaders may exist, and even be great at what they do on a functional level, such a weak dimension can't sustain the long-term health and survival of their tribe. These leaders are probably great in a manufacturing organization where they can manage from above instead of the distributed leadership model we see in the Service Age.

The foundation of the *Care : Compassion* dimension is probably formed in childhood; how we were socialized by our parents, in our classes, and within our other social environments. These lessons and experiences probably developed how well or poorly we express our empathetic impulses toward one another.

Empathy is what connects people from within and beyond the tribe. It's the path for exchanging shared values within our communities and with others. In a professional or formal setting, empathy helps build trust between colleagues, peers, and clients. Great service happens mostly when there is a shared sense of caring and compassion, especially in the service setting, where the service provider can solve the pain or meet the need of the client or partner. Since we are all service providers to the people in our lives, we are always faced with opportunities to extend our care and compassion to the people we serve. It just so happens that front-line workers in a manufacturing plant aren't paid to work with other people, but off the line even they provide personal service to their colleagues, bosses, family, friends and everyone else. If we adapt Roosevelt's message within this context, it's that people won't care what's in our other dimensions if we don't show that we care about what's in their 12 dimensions.

This dimension shows our ability to feel what someone else is feeling. Or, as the quote from the Cherokee tribe of Native Americans advises, "Don't judge a man until you have walked a mile in his shoes." The ability to reserve judgment and imagine ourselves in another person's life in order to get in touch with their feelings and ideas is the selfless component of this dimension. I firmly believe many of the failures in the corporate arena have happened because rewarding the few (executives and shareholders) is given priority over the welfare of everyone else.

That said, I'm not suggesting the answer is to prop up the kind of blind egalitarian social structures we see in today's Communist states. They seem to show no consideration for rewarding those who achieved excellence, compared to the meritocracy that says anyone who wants to achieve true success in service should get their fair turn, and part of that means ensuring the health and quality of their *Care : Compassion* dimension is good. Actually, what we've seen in practice is that Communist states are precisely lacking in care and compassion by treating everyone as if they are one-dimensional. This is understandable and to be expected, given that they were the result of upheavals born from the Industrial Age. Ultimately, however, the goal is to encourage authentic compassion for others as a path to elevate one's personal brand.

Other facets of this dimension include being other-centric as opposed to egocentric. Parents typically put the needs of their children far ahead of themselves, so imagine what an impact you would have in your career if that was your approach when you delivered personal service on the job? I'm not suggesting absolute selflessness, because a judicious amount of selfishness goes a long way, but in the Service Age, the needs of the served should be attended to by a caring server. That, after all, is part of the covenant built into the service moment.

In auditing our *Care : Compassion* dimension, we must remain as honest as possible. Convincing ourselves that we care about others when we're more interested in getting personal results or rewards isn't caring. Even if we fool ourselves, most people around us will see us for what we really are. Especially for this dimension, being inauthentic about how much we care and having a fake degree of compassion will be a clear signal to others to stay away – nothing could be less inspiring in a service leader.

To a large extent, either you care or you don't, but there are certainly ways of encouraging growth. Volunteering for a charity or a cause you believe in will put you in the trenches. That kind of sobering reminder of what's at stake and what's happening on the ground is a great way to inspire deep empathy.

Do not underestimate the power of selflessness – giving your time and energy to others without expectation of recognition or reward is extremely empowering and it will enhance your personal brand in ways you can't expect. If you're looking for a cause or a group to join, I suggest picking a small organization where your contribution will have a greater impact. Much as anonymous giving delivers deep satisfaction, the growth you feel will be more pronounced if your direct contribution can be felt immediately.

In a service setting, you can strengthen this dimension by

seeing the service moment as an opportunity when the other person has entered your life and can leave it feeling more enriched for having crossed your path. Increasing other people's satisfaction in what they do or are receiving delivers a large increase in our own satisfaction and wellbeing. A truly win-win situation.

ACTION!

STEP 1: TODAY   STEP 2: TOMORROW

THIS IS
WHERE I AM
WHO I AM
HOW I AM

ACTION

THIS IS
WHERE I WANT TO BE
WHO I WANT TO BE
HOW I WANT TO BE

APPLY, MODIFY AND REPEAT

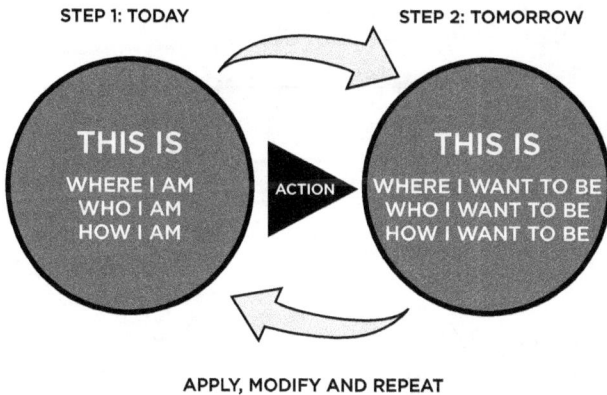

Review your *Care : Compassion* dimension and decide if it needs strengthening. This is the part of your personal brand that is probably the hardest to 'fake it 'till you make it', because if you ever faked being compassionate or having empathy, it would probably sabotage your efforts in the first place. Making a review of your dimension, it is easy to fall into the trap of self-deception. You may tell yourself that you care and have a healthy range of empathy and compassion for others, but you may actually be the opposite. Therefore, one good way to not fall into the trap is to get in the trenches – pick the battle that touches you and then jump in. If you've already found where you want to put your energy, so much the better. This might be the one dimension you would be best to get out of your head and mix with the troops.

Step 1: TODAY

Get a clear sense of your present situation. Write down the elements of your *Care : Compassion* dimension that affect where and how you live, work, and have fun in the different environments of your day-to-day world.

1. _____

2. _____

3. _____

4. _____

5 _____

Step 2: TOMORROW

Make an inventory of what you would like to be in the future. Although *Tomorrow* can literally mean tomorrow, it can also mean one or five years from now.

1. _____

2. _____

3. _____

4. _____

5. _____

Step 3: ACTION

Decide what you need to do to move from *Today* to *Tomorrow*. Define and carry out all actions great and small to

help move toward your goal.

1. _____

2. _____

3. _____

4. _____

5. _____

Step 4: APPLY, MODIFY, AND REPEAT

TOP CHEF IN ACTION - THE *CARE : COMPASSION* DIMENSION

When scouting locations for *Le Petit Plat*, Sharon understood that where she opened would either strengthen the location of an already established quarter or it would create a new one. Choosing the latter option because it would keep initial costs low, she soon discovered that the restaurant was a magnet for the poor and disadvantaged.

The first few months after opening were a big surprise - Sharon had no idea she would have to spend so much money and time repairing broken windows and upgrading the security system. The new fine-dining restaurant was a perfect target for burglary, and this pushed the new business to the breaking point.

Sharon understood that in order to free her business from this potentially life-threatening situation, the best way to deal with the problem was to tackle it face on. Every second Monday of the month, *Le Petit Plat* hosted special cooking classes for local residents only. In order to qualify for the free admission, participants had to show proof of residence. Then, once admitted on a first-come, first-served basis, Sharon and her sou-chef showed how anyone could create mouth-watering dishes on a budget.

By working directly with her neighbors and the local residents, Sharon's reputation grew. The more she gave to the community, the more the community gave back. Within a year, the vandalism and break-ins had stopped, and Sharon and her staff were considered champions in the community.

The *Social : Relationship* Dimension

Chapter Summary:
Managing your *Social : Relationship* dimension is one of the most powerful ways to build a following and a reputation as a connected, caring leader. Make sure you address how much you care about others, how attractive and energetic you are, and the elements within you that make you fun and pleasing to others in your network.

Typically, when people turn to you because they need you, a driving motivation is their self-interest. If you have strong functional abilities that can solve people's pains, they will probably turn to you. This satisfies basic needs, but the real depth of the *Social : Relationship* dimension is when people are in your life because you have social attraction and these people want an active relationship with you. Having a strong *Social : Relationship* dimension means you are engaging, funny, knowledgeable, fascinating, compassionate, and a contributor to the group's happiness. Strengthening this dimension can result in lifting the energy of the group through your influence and emotional intelligence.

Returning to Gad, he makes the argument that a brand's social dimension is what anchors brands to groups. Brands that have a strong social dimension are able to create strong affinities between customers and are themselves representative of each person's social identity. As he put it, "The brand quite often creates a cult around itself, it becomes a social insignia, a prop in the lifestyle play of an individual."

One good example of this power can be seen in the people who pick Starbucks over other coffee shops. Loyalty to the brand comes from functional qualities and the social dimension behind the brand. People self-select and segregate themselves based on their needs (the taste, choice and delivery of the coffee) and how they are served in their social dimension. Fitting into the right social group and cultivating strong relationships within the group happens as we are drawn to the one with social traits that are meaningful to us on personal and social levels.

This is important because having a clear sense of who you are and what motivates you can help you better manage your behaviors and expectations. Having a clear sense of your triggers can enhance your relationships and the feeling that you belong. This way, you can better contribute to your network's harmony, competitiveness (depending, of course, on the goals of the group), and your relationships within the network.

Your *Social : Relationship* dimension hinges on the notion of what's considered 'appropriate', a cue that brings social judgment from others. How well you read and adjust your behavior to connect with your groups will determine how much the group considers you a resource or a drain. The more that people in your social and professional circles find that you are behaving appropriately within a given situation, the more appreciated and valued you will be to the group. One immediate step you can work on in case you would like to enhance this dimension, is to learn a few funny, politically neutral and 'clean' jokes. Laughter is a great way to bring people together, so having a set of quality jokes that won't offend is always useful.

Making an audit of your *Social : Relationship* dimension will help you understand what in your behavior or attitude attracts or repels others. In an organization, strengthening this dimension means you will find ways to work better with and lead the members in your team. The strong relationships you build will get you through the challenging times that all businesses must overcome.

The danger of not having a strong *Social : Relationship* dimension is that you may push people away or people will drift apart from you, eventually making you an outcast. This may take a long time to happen, but once people have been pushed too far by your weak or under-developed dimension, there may be no going back.

This dimension is a good example of one that doesn't get considered on the production line. On an assembly line, the company is essentially buying your *Competence : Expertise* dimension through your labor. Your ability to exercise a strong Social : Relationship dimension may be negligible. If we look back at the founder of the production line, Henry Ford, and his legacy of making cars available for the masses, he broke down the big picture of production to basic units of production. Ford, and the majority of manufacturing companies after him, didn't leverage how well workers connected with others on the line as a business outcome. It doesn't matter, as long as the production quota is met. Whether the team is socially unified or not is not important, although that social unification probably comes after hours and off the line. In a service setting, however, this dimension is precisely what cultivates the connection clients feel within a company and its services. We are social animals and this dimension must be cultivated for us to be fully dimensional in everything we do.

The most important step is to identify and limit the habits that can turn people off. Although people may consciously recognize and reward positive qualities that build social harmony – a great trait in any manager – they will consistently avoid someone who has the toxic traits in them.

A common example is if someone has the habit of using discriminatory language and behavior. Even if it's tolerated for a while, it's likely that the person, over the long term, will eventually get rejected. Again, even if it doesn't happen for a long time, this person is a ticking time bomb; collective patience will probably run out. People would just prefer to work within a team that doesn't have a toxic or volatile dynamic.

For all relationships, improving social dexterity to better serve the people around us can be a great source of growth and strength. One example of this social dexterity is how well and often we make an effort to help people feel welcome and comfortable. Or how well we avoid putting people on the spot and embarrassing them over what might be an insecurity.

Imagine someone who is highly detail-oriented and an accomplished problem solver. The *Social : Relationship* dimension for this person when they're doing the nuts and bolts of their job probably doesn't need to be especially developed. For example, a reclusive engineer can be quite successful if his or her designs are innovative and of the highest quality. But, if the time comes when he or she wants to move up the ladder into management, not having a strong dimension will have a direct impact on how well he or she can motivate the team to complete a project. Although his or her technical and competence may be top-notch, once he or she moves into management – a service role – something like his or her *Social : Relationship* dimension can make all the difference. Let's compare this example with a physician or a lawyer. Unless this professional is the expert without equal, it's the user-friendly ones – the ones with the strong Social : Relationship dimension – that will be more successful.

With this dimension, both the person and the group are affecting one another. When people find themselves ejected from the group, the desire generally crops up to migrate to another group. In other words, we tend to match our social requirements to groups of people who match our social needs. The people who go to Starbucks are a little bit different in their social profile from those who hang out at Pacific Coffee or the independent coffee shop. The social environment and group qualities themselves are enough to attract other like-minded customers.

From a branding perspective, you want people to self-select as part of your brand. This is particularly important when you're aiming for repeat interactions. Where the server is the service, it follows that even when buying a product, customers are first buying the salesperson. For example, if you're shopping for a laptop, how well the salesperson delivers the service can decide if you go through the sales process and come back when you need a new machine. Customers will often show loyalty to people and products that are socially aligned with their own values, habits and personal brand.

When a person's *Social : Relationship* dimension is corrupted, the people in that person's network will eventually avoid being with the person. At worst, the offensive person becomes a social pariah. In the same way that rude and foul-mouthed people who swear all the time can make others feel uncomfortable; it can literally drain the energy from the relationship.

A review of your dimension should include how you use social media platforms like Facebook, Twitter and LinkedIn. These are good tools if you have a knack for it, but having many friends, fans or followers in social media are artifacts of having a strong Social : Relationship dimension. The skill of building a following happens when you have an attractive social media 'voice' and tone for how you share your ideas and experience. That said, you can have a strong dimension without cultivating a large social media following. One does not limit the other.

Remember that you're a hub in your social network and having a strong dimension means you won't turn people off; you have the skills to communicate the quality of your multidimensional self. Cultivating your relationships through this dimension – online and offline – demands that you think about and adjust the ways you integrate with others. Are you a user-friendly person? Are you a source of strength, support and resources, even when you have to say no?

One way to strengthen this dimension is by working on your appeal, which includes how well you project presence, power and warmth. By presence, it's what happens when you enter a room or a conversation. When your dimension is strong, you are welcomed as an active participant, even if you're not controlling what's happening between people. Sometimes people who lack a healthy Social : Relationship dimension try to control others and this comes off as bossy; but no one would confuse bossiness with being socially captivating. Next, by projecting power, this means that people around you sense you're not about to shy away from stepping forward, be it in conversation or in action. Rounding it off is the projection of warmth, which is the authentic expression of caring about everyone in the room, even those who disagree with you or are in competition with you. Exercising this dimension is a skill, something that everyone can work on. For starters, being aware of your strengths and managing your behavior to improve how well you project presence, power and warmth will greatly enhance your appeal. Another good start is to limit the behaviors that dilute your expression of these three elements.

One more skill you can develop to build up your *Social : Relationship* dimension is to get good at storytelling. Listen to any US presidential speech or anyone else in a leading position, and you will most often find that a message's power and presence is conveyed through story. When it comes to this dimension, the one who tells the best story wins.

If you develop an awareness and appreciation of others in your social groups who have qualities you admire, develop these strengths in yourself by quietly mirroring these people. It's likely that the people you know with greatest social dexterity are probably not in the habit of offending others within the group. This is a little self-evident – that the popular people don't repel people within their network – but the point is to stress that good service leaders have learned to express themselves in ways that don't antagonize the members of their team, group or tribe. Definitely have an opinion, but maybe tone down how opinionated you are; or share your ambition, but not in a way that's seen as aggressive. To take some inspiration from Buddhism and Confucianism, it's best to take the middle of the road.

One practical task you can use to build your *Social : Relationship* dimension is to gather a collection of five or six 'clean' but truly funny jokes. This will create a good-mood enhancer in social situations and you will be appreciated for adding to the group's upbeat energy and social health. It's not that service leaders have to lose their sense of humor, but that the larger the group and the higher the stakes, the more important it is to keep jokes, stories, and off-the-cuff remarks under control. There are many examples of people at the top who did serious damage to their credibility and personal brand simply because they made a joke or comment that went down like a lead balloon. So part of refining and strengthening this dimension is understanding how to read a group, how to engage among them (one-on-one or in total), and reigning in any behaviors that might destroy trust.

On a deeper level, improving the strength of this dimension should include increasing the amount of compassion you have. If you don't authentically care about others, you're not going to fool anyone in the long term. This, too, can end up repelling others. I often hear people questioning the usefulness and effect of self-interest on a group's cohesion. In my experience I have found that self-interest is just one area under the *Social : Relationship* dimension. It is useful to strengthen this dimension and improve your personal brand for the service of others so that you are valued as someone who enhances the interests of the group. Developing skills so you can help others is the right thing, but developing skills so you can take advantage of others isn't. If you are not cultivating yourself to better help others, people will eventually see you as manipulative, dedicated to your own success and reward over the wellbeing of others.

How strong you are will directly result in how well you attract people to you, especially in the Social : Relationship dimension. It's no accident that a socially attractive person who is a great friend will draw others, purely because people want to be part of a strong social circle. That he or she has a good habit of self-reflection to spot the weaknesses in their dimensions only enhances their personal brand and helps this service leader be even more attractive or inspiring to others.

What's most interesting about this dimension is that it's a part of you which you can address right away and with relatively little effort. Similar to discovering what makes you happy by identifying what makes you unhappy, this dimension can be directly improved by reducing the toxic or viral qualities that may be corrupting it. Stopping toxic behaviors like being rude, abrasive or exaggerating to the point of dishonesty immediately cleans up the viruses that may have been corrupting your personal brand. Other milder forms of these negative stains on your personal brand can include how moody you are, if you're always late, if you continually let others pay bills, if you're argumentative or negative, or if you're always exhausted because you can't say no.

It's also important to understand the differences between behaviors that are unsocial or amoral – which have their place – compared to behaviors that are antisocial and immoral. Some behaviors connected with solitude and avoiding social interactions aren't necessarily toxic or negative. Service leaders must also be able to live and thrive in solitude, such as if a person needs to withdraw and disconnect from others in order to recharge. On the other hand, there are behaviors that are antisocial and immoral, and they go against the moral grain in a social group and are toxic. The developed service leader can thrive within these subtle but crucial differences.

Since the *Social : Relationship* dimension is so woven with how you relate to others, a good barometer to gauge this dimension is to look at what people around you are saying. Be attentive to yourself, your friends and your work for cues that you're overly committed to this dimension. If you put too much energy in your *Social : Relationship* dimension, like going out drinking with clients too much, it can drag on your *Economic : Security* or *Physical : Health* dimensions. The chances are, your friends and associates will let you know if this is the case.

If you're actively trying to build your leadership momentum, remember that the more you attract others through your strong *Social : Relationship* dimension, the closer they will get to you - and this isn't always a good thing. For example, if you have a lot of money, more people will want to spend time with you to get more of almost anything from you. As you attract a greater following, be aware that you can manage how many to include in your network and how close they can get to you. Ultimately, you must set your comfort zone and the strategy that works best for you. By doing this you will expand your network and people will see you as a hub for things or services, without the risk of being taken advantage of or potentially exploited. In time, you will barter with others, especially on things money can't buy.

One good example of this is the extra mile. We all pay for products and services, but you can't pay for the extra mile you get when people are deeply connected to you. Having a strong Social : Relationship dimension can help win that extra mile from people.

In Asia, and certainly with how business people think things work in mainland China, much has been said around the idea and influence of *guanxi*, which refers to how Asian businesses seem limited to the strength of direct relationships. Although it sounds exotic, I don't see *guanxi* as so different from the relationship building or networking seen in other cultures. Go to Wall Street and see how far you'll get if your *Social : Relationship* dimension isn't developed. It may not get the headlines, but the importance of relationships and relationship building is just as important in the West as it is in Asia. Also, it's always important to be aware of how you are using your connections. Are you using them to get in line or are you using them to jump ahead of everyone else? One action – the butting in line of course – will easily stand out as toxic to others.

Finally, let's remember once again that service is social. People are social animals, so if you want to get ahead as a people-person who is well connected, you better make sure you're practising the skills and habits of a healthy, inspiring social animal.

ACTION!

THIS IS
WHERE I AM
WHO I AM
HOW I AM

ACTION

THIS IS
WHERE I WANT TO BE
WHO I WANT TO BE
HOW I WANT TO BE

APPLY, MODIFY AND REPEAT

Review your *Social : Relationship* dimension and decide if it needs strengthening. This is the part of your personal brand that is most directly related to your personal service. Make an honest review of your dimension and consider what an upgrade could mean and look like. For this dimension, you will need to review how appealing you are, your level of empathy, how well you connect with and support others, and how wide or narrow your social connections are. Your Social : Relationship dimension deeply affects your personal and professional lives and can reveal the path toward greater success and achievement – remember that service leadership is ultimately the result of how well or poorly you connect with others.

Step 1: TODAY

Get a clear sense of your present situation. Write down the elements of your *Social : Relationship* dimension that affect the people in your life, where you live, work, and have fun in the different environments of your day-to-day world.

1. _____

2. _____

3. _____

4. _____

5. _____

Step 2: TOMORROW

Make an inventory of what you would like to be in the future. Although *Tomorrow* can literally mean tomorrow, it can also mean one or five years from now.

1. _____

2. _____

3. _____

4. _____

5. _____

Step 3: ACTION

Decide what you need to do to move from *Today* to *Tomorrow*. Define and carry out all actions, great and small, to help move toward your goal.

1. _____

2. _____

3. _____

4. _____

5. _____

Step 4: APPLY, MODIFY, AND REPEAT

TOP CHEF IN ACTION – THE *SOCIAL : RELATIONSHIP* DIMENSION

Sharon is proud of her ability to draw a crowd into her restaurant. This is not only because the food is of the highest quality, but also because she has broadened the loyalty of diners who consider her restaurant among the best in the city.

Sharon's *Social : Relationship* dimension is what lets her relate to her customers and her team. As her staff has come to know her, her people have come to appreciate that she's as loyal to them as they are to her. Ultimately, the success and reputation the restaurant has won are the results of Sharon's ability to connect with people and form strong relationships.

Sharon wasn't always like this. When she started in the business, especially when she was apprenticing in Paris, she learned the hard way how important it was to build good relationships with everyone. At first her French was rusty and she would often irritate the other cooks. It was a lonely time for her because she couldn't relate to her colleagues due to the language barrier. Over weeks and months, French classes helped improve her speech and she was able to win over the staff. Also, her sincere and open attitude made a huge difference. She soon earned the enthusiastic support from the head chef.

Sharon doesn't consider herself outgoing or the life of the party, but she knows that once she walks into the restaurant she has to inspire everyone with her energy, competence, warmth and ability to relate to customers, suppliers and everyone else.

Chapter
EIGHT

The *Visual : Daily Management* Dimension

Chapter Summary:
This dimension involves how others view the way you dress, your style, and physical presentation. It also includes the habits you keep, whether around hygiene or other daily routines that keep you looking good and acceptable for the role you are in.

In the previous chapters, we dealt with the different ways that you show care, empathy and unselfish behavior, and some effects these may have on your social networks. Now we'll get more 'superficial' and review the *Visual : Daily Management* dimension. This dimension covers what you look like and how your physical self comes across. Although it may seem frivolous, remember that in branding, packaging is more than half the product. Many of our conscious and subconscious attachments to commercial and personal brands are based on what we see.

By our *Visual : Daily Management* dimension, I'm talking about what we look like, be it the clothes we wear, our hair style, choice of accessories, and everything else that we can link to our fashion. This look-good feel-good attitude also includes whether we have bad breath, bad body odor, or other physical attributes that put people off when we're serving others and how well we follow norms that are expected in a given situation.

This is worth reviewing because it's in our best interest to have the kind of presentation that reinforces our personal brand. Moreover, if we remember the Anna Karenina Principle, we need to find and purge whichever bad elements we have in us that may harm our effectiveness or lead to our failure.

We want people to see an accurate or defined reflection of who we are, what we do, and what we aspire to become. This consistency helps reinforce the message or projection of influence we may be aiming for and can work in our favor when we deal with people who judge us because of what we look like. Whether we like it or not, if we don't manage what we look like and we have a physical presentation that isn't strong, this can put barriers up that stop us even before we step through the door. Some people we may want to work with may even dismiss us based on something as seemingly trivial as how well we dress.

In managing my own dimension, I found the book *10 Steps to Fashion Freedom: Discover Your Personal Style from the Inside Out* by Malcolm Levene and Kate Mayfield useful.[11] They suggest a shortcut to help sharpen one's wardrobe. To do it, simply pick a Hollywood movie star that is most aligned with your own strategy and aesthetic, and then mirror that person. They can be mentors for their style and you will benefit simply by mimicking how they dress and present themselves to the public.

I couldn't be a Gary Cooper or Brad Pitt, but Paul Newman was someone who was a source of inspiration. I took him as a role model and, from him, built my own visual style. I made an inventory of what he wore in different situations and began to do it myself.

These stars are in the business of leveraging and cultivating a style that matches their personal brand; standing apart from other celebrities in order to stand out to the public. Rather than making myself into a Paul Newman lookalike, this source of inspiration should form a foundation for my own style. There's no reason why this couldn't also work for you. Remember that stars have professional stylists whose job is to carefully craft their clients' look for maximum effect. By mimicking a star's style, we benefit from the creative effort these celebrity stylists and consultants offer. There's no shame in standing on the shoulders of giants, so feel free to use these shortcuts as a way to stand on the shoulders of your style giants.

To refine one's stylistic literacy a little more, fashion designers separate people (their target market) in order to better serve them. No item of clothing will appeal to or look good on everyone, so designers create collections that target groups. How designers do this is by the color of people's hair and their skin tone – these are the 'seasons' some people talk about. Depending on your skin tone, eyes, and hair color, you will fall under a matching season. These include Dark Autumn, Cool Winter, and Light Spring. For example, American actress Jennifer Aniston is considered a 'Soft Summer' and she will typically choose soft, cool colors since they look best on her.

To narrow down your own season, if you have warm skin undertones (for example, the veins under your skin look green) you are probably a Spring or an Autumn. Winters and Summers have cool skin undertones so their veins look blue. People who have warm skin, eyes and hair are either Warm Autumn or Warm Spring. If you have cool tones you are either a Cool Winter or Cool Summer. If you have strong, dark features you have a 'dark' season. To get an accurate fix on your own type, there are many resources online and shops where you can go to figure out your season. You can even hire a color analyst to do it for you. By knowing your season you can build up your wardrobe in ways that heighten your strengths.

If you question how useful this is, either for yourself or in the business world, consider the late Steve Jobs, the legendary co-founder of Apple. Jobs had a personal brand that eventually became strictly about jeans and a black turtleneck. This was such a part of his brand that imagine what the headlines would have been like had he shown up at a product launch wearing a suit and tie. Regardless of the product's features, his new way of dressing the part as Apple's leader would have been the news story, not the new iPhone or any other state-of-the-art product. When he headed the world's most profitable company, it's not as if he couldn't afford a suit, but the jeans and turtleneck were signature elements of his *Visual : Daily Management* dimension.

If you're stepping into an environment where there's already a loose or strict uniform, you're entering a place that already has its team identity and you need to fit its visual dimension. Just match your own visual presentation to what's already there. You can bend the rules a little if you want but this could come off as unprofessional. If your aim is to command or get others to trust you from the start, it helps if you have the right visual cues on your side.

Back in the early 1970s when I was launching DHL, I wanted to be seen as a fashionable courier. At the time, this meant having broad lapels on my suit jacket and a broad tie with some pretty outrageous colors. I was hardly dressed like a hippie, but I was following the fashion hallmarks that were trendy at the time. At first, no one – and I do mean no one – gave me the time of day. Here I was, trying to get people to trust a courier company that could literally save their companies millions of dollars but I had no takers. I was complaining about this to a friend when he suggested that I dress like an IBM salesman. The conservative heads at the banks and shipping executives were looking for trust – the kind the blue-suited IBM salespeople were renowned for representing. The suit reinforced this message of trust, so I gave it a try – I had nothing to lose. That little change made all the difference. I closed three deals in one week. That's all it took.

For a more current example, Facebook founder Mark Zuckerberg has his own signature brand. At a press conference or a new product launch, he'll wear a grey hoodie or t-shirt with jeans. That's good when he's being the press-friendly 'face of Facebook', but when he's meeting with investors or US president Barack Obama, his visual presentation changes to match the occasion. This is out of respect, or to most effectively align with the group. Likewise, when I'm invited to see a government leader, the expectation and situation demands that I put on a suit.

To use another example of how something as trivial as color can have a major effect on your life, I'll describe a time when I once bought the wrong-colored car. This was many years ago, long after I had established for myself and my personal brand that when it came to projecting the aura I wanted, I felt I needed to stick to deep, rich blue tones. This was true for how I dressed and other 'iconic' features. When the time came to get a new car, I went to the dealer and I picked out the car that was right for me. Since I was ordering it and was getting some custom options, the question of color came up and I mistakenly placed an order for a silver model. I waited three months until the car was delivered and then realized within a few days that I had made a costly mistake. For years I had always stuck to blue cars - and have ever since - but that was the one time when I let the salesperson get the better of me. I only needed to make that mistake once to learn my lesson.

With regard to the daily management side of this dimension, this includes all the habits you must maintain to have a strong presentation. It involves personal hygiene, good eating and drinking habits, getting enough sleep, and all the other behaviors that influence how people see you. A business owner or manager who looks slovenly, and has bad breath or bad body odor, will slowly but surely repel the people in his or her network. If a person with a weak dimension is at a position of service leadership, this is a strong example where the Anna Karenina Principle will kick in. In time, the team will fall apart out of being literally repulsed by the service leader.

How to review your own *Visual : Daily Management* dimension is to find somebody who fits your strategy, model yourself after this person, and build up your visual element to communicate your values and brand character in a way that is consistent. Similarly, there are many resources that list or clarify good habits for maintaining strong daily management. Keep in mind that part of daily management is maintaining your mindful persistence or the grit I mentioned in Chapter 2 – *You Are Your Personal Brand.*

Let's say that you review your visual dimension and decide that you need a bit of a makeover or better ingredients to improve your visual presentation. This might mean going over what's in your closet, the state of your hair, and what your teeth look like. Although some might think that building up a better wardrobe takes a pile of money, it doesn't. You can easily find expensive clothes that will set you back some serious cash, but it doesn't have to be that way. A small set of well-chosen, reasonably-priced clothes will do the trick.

None of this is about burying your personality in order to look like one of the herd. If part of your personal brand is about expressing yourself in how you dress, then that is the part you should follow. Just be aware that your *Visual : Daily Management* dimension is a factor that can either add to or rob from your personal brand.

ACTION!

STEP 1: TODAY   STEP 2: TOMORROW

THIS IS

WHERE I AM
WHO I AM
HOW I AM

ACTION

THIS IS

WHERE I WANT TO BE
WHO I WANT TO BE
HOW I WANT TO BE

APPLY, MODIFY AND REPEAT

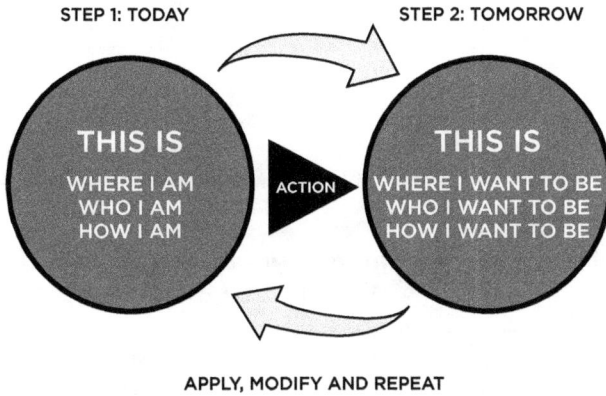

Review your *Visual : Daily Management* dimension and decide if it needs strengthening. Remember that this is the part of your personal brand that drives a large part of your impression on others. Although it's explicitly superficial, it can significantly impact your path to success. Make a deep, honest review of what you might need to modify or adapt. For example, can you really say that you dress the part you play in your group? Are your daily habits supporting a physical and physiological presentation that portrays your role to the fullest? It helps to explore in depth your style, personal hygiene, and other factors that may attract or repel others.

Step 1: TODAY
Get a clear sense of your present situation. Write down the elements of your *Visual : Daily Management* dimension that affect where and how you live, work, and have fun in the different environments of your day-to-day world.

1. _____

2. _____

3. _____

4. _____

5. _____

Step 2: TOMORROW
Make an inventory of what you would like to be in the future. Although *Tomorrow* can literally mean tomorrow, it can also mean one or five years from now.

1. _____

2. _____

3. _____

4. _____

5. _____

Step 3: ACTION
Decide what you need to do to move from *Today* to *Tomorrow*. Define and carry out all actions, great and small, to help move toward your goal.

1. _____

2. _____

3. _____

4. _____

5. _____

Step 4: APPLY, MODIFY, AND REPEAT

TOP CHEF IN ACTION – THE *VISUAL : DAILY MANAGEMENT* DIMENSION

When Sharon worked with the architect to design the interior of *Le Petit Plat*, it was critical for the kitchen to include a section that was open to diners. Once open and running, customers always had a view of the kitchen staff at work. Communicating the importance of this standard to her staff was critical. If the restaurant was about conveying the best ingredients served under the best conditions, everything and everyone had to be top-of-the-class.

Sharon was detail oriented and it showed in how she worked. The food that came out of her kitchen and how she dressed consistently sent the message of refined taste and style. She made it a point that her own chef's wardrobe was immaculate and stylish, and she insisted this also carried over to everyone on staff, even the dishwashers. She understood that everything about how the team looked needed to be consistent with the commitment to quality.

She was known for being a stickler for excellence. Although she didn't single people out to embarrass them, it wasn't beyond her to pull one of her waiters aside to point out that he had overdone it on the cologne one night or that one of her line-cooks had an apron that was too stained and a fresh apron was needed right away. The point was to never turn off the customers because of something so basic as hygiene.

The *Emotional : Happiness* Dimension

Chapter Summary:
This dimension is about designing a way that works for you to minimize your pains, find harmony in your emotional state, and raise your level of personal happiness. By doing so, you will attract others to your uplifting energy and personal brand.

This dimension is as rich, varied and diverse as the *Competence : Expertise* dimension; everything we do thrives or crumbles, depending on our emotional state. There are many emotions that may be driving us and you may need to focus on managing specific emotions within you. You can get far by simply being self-aware, but a good barometer of how well you're doing is the feedback you get from people around you. I won't go into all the ingredients that make up our *Emotional : Happiness* dimension, but if you suspect you have serious issues to deal with, professional help is worth exploring. There's no shame in it. Counseling, psychotherapy and related services certainly have their place. It would be naïve to think that all leaders are emotional rocks, but the true service leader owns his or her mental states, can feel and process their vulnerabilities, and finds practical strategies to manage these states. For convenience, and to keep the discussion flowing, I'll use the catch-all notion of wellbeing and happiness to refer to the optimal state when looking at this dimension.

I'm focusing on wellbeing, although our *Emotional : Happiness* dimension is far richer. For some people, they're at their best when they have the edge of stress pushing them forward. Others seek or create conflict around themselves in order to find the fuel to move forward. We wouldn't describe these people as happy, but, for them, conflict and turbulence fulfill a need that brings satisfaction. For example, a parent may find that their child consistently argues and resists when the underlying motivation is a desire to establish an emotional connection. Being a parent really is a solid building block and battleground for service leadership, and managing a child's tantrums or sudden bursts of conflicting emotions is great service leadership training (even if it can make your hair turn grey).

By wellbeing and happiness, I don't only mean the sense of joy we feel when something goes well – although that's a great state to be in. Instead, I mean the many different emotions we experience when we're feeling good, positive or in an optimal state.

This is the dimension that you can do well to 'fake it until you make it', even if you're not feeling up to it. It's unrealistic to think we can design a life where we're always on a high of unspoiled happiness. You may be in a blissful state for a while, but all things must pass. Who among us would say they've never experienced pain or unhappiness? The Buddhist attitude, for example, is that life cannot avoid suffering. A review of this dimension isn't about finding the magic trick to achieve never-ending happiness, but to encourage you to develop strategies that increase how often and how long you remain happy. The greatest benefit is that the happier you are, the more people around you will be uplifted. Rather than dragging down the energy, it's much better to lift the energy of the room and even be the life of the party. Happiness and optimism can be infectious, much the same as unhappiness and pessimism can infect and spread like a virus throughout your network.

In a service moment, it's clear that the happier the server is, the better and more impactful the service will be. For those who have worked a service job in retail, a common expectation is that the server leaves his or her personal problems at the door. The moment the server enters the role, his or her face and mood are the company they represent. For the more analytical type of person who never considered what it means to be a service provider, this may sound soft or vague. A chemist or meteorologist might find explorations of this dimension frivolous, especially around his or her level of happiness. This may work if you're in a lab or reviewing meteorological models and data, but once you have to deal with other people, this dimension can make all the difference. The Anna Karenina Principle can bring down your castle if you leave this dimension neglected.

There are definite, clear advantages and effects on a group's quality of engagement and bottom line when a team is made up of happy people. Whether you're in the executive suite or on the front line, being emotionally stable and happy enhances productivity. At a minimum, a team whose members manage their *Emotional : Happiness* dimension will connect more strongly with other team members and clients.

In our book on entrepreneurship, Saimond Ip and I discussed how the founder's emotional state sets the tone for everyone in the tribe.[4] If the founder has toxic qualities and a bad disposition, this will be a big hurdle for people behind the start-up. Toxic qualities will seep into our *Emotional : Happiness* dimension and we can end up dragging down the emotional state of people around us.

When I've mentored students and others who wanted to

be better entrepreneurs, I have specifically addressed the person's emotions. I asked these budding entrepreneurs how happy they were and why they thought it was critical for the start-up. For some, they were so high on their *Competence : Expertise* dimension and low on their *Emotional : Happiness* dimension that it threw all their other dimensions off balance. To help these entrepreneurs succeed, I needed to help them manage their emotional states and the idea of their own happiness.

The best way to understand what happiness is, is to appreciate the absence of unhappiness. Some students have argued that this is meaningless wordplay but let it sit for a moment to explore the insights that are here.

First, make an inventory; list the things, large and small, that make you unhappy and see if you can reduce the frequency and power they have in your life. For example, most of my deepest unhappiness used to come from other people. After recognizing this, I decided to give them all a free pass; I forgave them for what they had consciously or inadvertently done to me. I managed this by myself and in the comfort of my own space. It was enough to free myself from a lot of the tension and unhappiness I had been dragging behind me like an anchor – things I had been carrying for years.

To use a fisheries-based example, imagine you have an aquarium in your head with ideas and experiences swimming around like goldfish and electric eels. If you bring the two species to the surface of your thoughts and touch them, you get two kinds of jolts; the goldfish gives you a little rush and the eel gives you a shock. The eels are the people and experiences that bring unhappiness, and we all have triggers that bring them to the surface. These triggers can shock us at any time, like in the middle of giving a speech. *ZAP!* A jolt of unhappiness or pain.

Now imagine using a strategy that minimizes how often you bring the eels to the surface. That would minimize the jolts. My advice is that the first step toward happiness is to limit the things that bring you unhappiness. To do that you must first really understand what your eels are. How old are they? Where did they come from? Who or what do they represent? What would happen if you killed them from neglect?

This model is no substitute for real psychotherapy or pharmacological treatment if it's called for, but it was my strategy for reducing and removing the thoughts that brought me unhappiness. The result? I became a happier person. With that out of the way, you can start reaching small goals each day, goals that together result in a rolling sense of accomplishment. If you want to build on your momentum of happiness, build on the success of your small goals after you minimize the barriers that bring you unhappiness. In other words, this was happiness *by design.*

Systematically identifying what makes you unhappy – those energy-sapping eels – and reducing their sting lets you focus your energy and attention on thoughts and activities that enhance your quality of life. The chances are, no great epiphanies will come after going through this process. This exercise is about raising awareness of what's going on within you, and by doing this you'll clarify what makes you unhappy, reduce the eels' power, and strengthen your *Emotional : Happiness* dimension. I did this for myself a few years ago and found that my emotional fulfillment lay mostly in forgiving people; burying the hatchet and moving on to the things I loved doing, such as painting, community service, and exploring the nature of service leadership.

In *The How of Happiness: A New Approach to Getting the Life You Want*, research psychologist and University of California professor of psychology Sonja Lyubomirsky explains how to increase happiness in your life.[12] She notes that we can all do big things that will make us happy, but we can also do little things that make us happy. The insight is that the amount of happiness we get – and by amount I mean the duration – is about the same. The idea is that if, for example, we get something for $1 or something for $500, although the functional benefits might change a lot, the actual duration of happiness that we derive from each is about the same. Lyubomirsky suggests that instead of focusing on getting or doing one big thing, and potentially waiting or denying yourself other joys in order to get it, do something smaller. The amount of happiness will be about the same, but cumulatively you will come out on top by having little highs more often.

I suggest spending 10 to 15 minutes every morning to map out your day, to fit in as many small joys as possible. The act of planning it out and consciously scheduling where you put your energy will nudge you in the right direction and slowly but surely free you from what can bring you down. Moreover, another facet of this is that ethical people can probably be called happier, when all's said and done. Doing the right thing may not make you break out into song and dance, because often doing the right thing can actually be a tough moment of crisis. Nevertheless, doing the right thing as a conscious state – no matter how grim the action that follows the decision – will leave you standing with your head held high, and this will bring a satisfaction and 'happiness' that can't be overstated.

Another insight worth considering comes from Mihaly Csikszentmihalyi, the former head of the Department of Psychology at the University of Chicago. He's a leading researcher in the study of happiness and his ideas have changed many people's lives. One core theory is that we can consciously bring up positive states through "flow" experiences.[13] These so-called flow experiences come when we take on a task that challenges us at the right level; just hard enough that we feel focused while doing it and the payoff feels great when the challenge is completed. If the task is too easy or too hard, engagement suffers and you'll miss out on your flow state because you're bored or frustrated. Flow activities can come from many sources, but if you can work them into your day, you will increase your sense of engagement, fulfillment and happiness.

There's a growing camp that argues that even if chasing flow experiences might help you feel good, it isn't necessarily a recipe for success. As Cal Newport explains in *So Good They Can't Ignore You: Why Skills Trump Passion in the Quest for Work You Love*, having and focusing on early-life passions isn't the norm and it probably isn't the right approach for everyone.[14] Instead, Newport suggests strengthening your "rare and valuable" skills in order to develop yourself into a "craftsman," and this focus can lead to a successful career. He asserts that in order to improve and grow, we must deliberately push ourselves beyond our comfort zone, or whatever level we need to be in a flow state. In other words, we are more likely to succeed when we look beyond our passions and focus on what we're actually good at doing. Then, through mastery, we can come out ahead of the pack. After we've been battle tested, we can explore our passions in a more leisurely fashion.

I propose that for many of us, an effective strategy for managing our Emotional : Happiness dimension is to clarify what happiness means for us, what elements work or don't, and focus on bringing in more positive experiences. I'm convinced that if you do this you will inspire people around you with an infectious, uplifting and appealing personal brand.

ACTION!

STEP 1: TODAY   STEP 2: TOMORROW

THIS IS   ACTION   **THIS IS**

WHERE I AM   WHERE I WANT TO BE
WHO I AM   WHO I WANT TO BE
HOW I AM   HOW I WANT TO BE

APPLY, MODIFY AND REPEAT

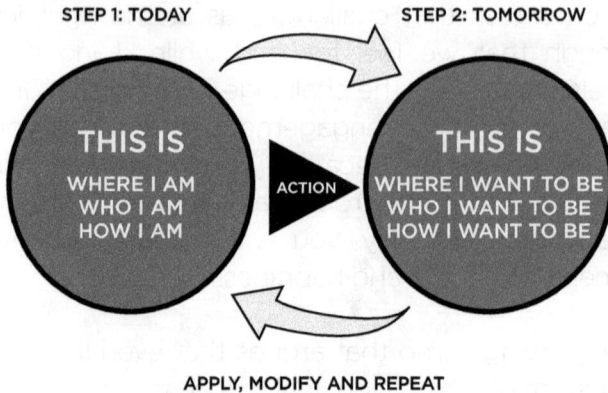

Review your *Emotional : Happiness* dimension and decide if it needs strengthening. This is the part of your personal brand that will attract others the most – there's nothing like someone uplifting to make everyone's day. Make an honest review of your dimension and consider making some changes. Imagine, for example, that there are people in your team that make you miserable. Is this enough to impact the quality of work you deliver and how you relate to others? Clearly, an improvement on this dimension will have a significant, direct impact on your life. One way of increasing your level of happiness is to identify the specific things that bring about tensions and why they make you unhappy. Remember that behind each negative emotion is an event or pattern of events that triggers certain thoughts inside you, and those thoughts are causing your unhappiness.

Step 1: TODAY
Get a clear sense of your present situation. Write down the elements of your *Emotional : Happiness* dimension that affect where and how you live, work, and have fun in the different environments of your day-to-day world. This not only includes what brings you happiness but also what brings you stress, tension, and unhappiness.

1. _____

2. _____

3. _____

4. _____

5. _____

Step 2: TOMORROW
Make an inventory of what you would like to be in the future. Although *Tomorrow* can literally mean tomorrow, it can also mean one or five years from now.

1. _____

2. _____

3. _____

4. _____

5. _____

Step 3: ACTION
Decide what you need to do to move from *Today* to *Tomorrow*. Define and carry out all actions, great and small, to help move toward your goal.

1. _____

2. _____

3. _____

4. _____

5. _____

Step 4: APPLY, MODIFY, AND REPEAT

TOP CHEF IN ACTION – THE *EMOTIONAL : HAPPINESS* DIMENSION

Le Petit Plat was always a hub of movement. From the moment the doors opened in the morning, Sharon and her staff would attend to all the details that made the restaurant special. One observation Sharon was especially proud of was when a reviewer noted that everyone in the restaurant was beaming, even in the thick of their evening dinner service.

Sharon made happiness within the restaurant a state she designed into the nature of the relationships and procedures. It wasn't that she insisted everyone smiled to customers and move with purpose and focus, but that there was a priority in the restaurant that it was a place where her staff wanted to be. Sharon was persistent about pushing her staff. She was demanding enough to make each shift a challenge, but she also ensured everyone was supported and had what they needed to deliver their best. In this climate, if someone lagged or tripped up to cause errors, everyone was in it for everyone else and the mistakes were corrected. Everyone could make mistakes, everyone could have a bad day. To maintain this climate of happiness, the team would have meetings to exchange war stories from the past week, what the mistakes were, and what might be the best solutions.

Sharon understood that by taking out the negative influences–either weeding out the wrong employees who brought people down or cutting out procedures that went against the team's harmony, she could make the restaurant into a great environment. Everyone would be proud of their work and each plate that came out of their kitchen, night after night.

Chapter
TEN

The *Mental : Intellectual* Dimension

Chapter Summary:
This dimension covers how you think about and explore the reasons behind things that affect you, the people around you, and how the world works. The best way to strengthen this dimension is to be curious about what's around you and try to encourage this curiosity with the people in your life. It also helps if you remain intellectually humble so that other people's ideas and opinions get their fair share of consideration when you make decisions.

This dimension includes your intelligence and your ability to think critically and logically. It forms the part of your awareness that lets you acquire and evaluate information. It also involves being able to debate ideas with others or internally, and even form hypotheses and thought experiments that test new ideas. This reflection is you at your intellectual best and it's important to have a strong dimension because it will let you connect with other people who problem-solve. With others, and this is especially important in a service environment when a new challenge emerges, you can explore how to find a solution to an unforeseen challenge. It's not that you need a high IQ, but more that you can exercise your mind to engage ideas of a higher level. If you would like a shortcut for how to strengthen this dimension, be an actively curious person and seek answers when questions crop up. Note that service hubs are the cities and regions that attract the multi-talented people who can see themselves thriving in that environment. To show the dynamics of service hubs and how they are influenced by each service leader's *Mental : Intellectual* dimension, consider the town of Nashville, Tennessee, in the USA.

In the history of American music, there aren't many cities that have stood out or been as important as Nashville. It doesn't matter to our discussion whether you like country music or not, because what's important is that the city has been the kind of service habitat that has attracted all the people who could contribute to the music industry. From composers to singers, performers to sound engineers, the city established itself as one of the most important places for anyone wanting to deliver the service of great music performance. As Nashville's music scene developed, thanks to the influence of Elvis Presley and the famed Grand Ole Opry among others, it attracted increasing numbers of service leaders. Nashville isn't where it is today only because people like Roy Orbison or Taylor Swift came here to launch their careers, but because it also attracted the lawyers, bankers, industry professionals, suppliers and everyone else involved in the music and entertainment sector. In order to innovate and deliver the world-class service needed to really excel, each person's *Mental : Intellectual* dimension had to have the quality that would enable this growth and innovation.

One of the most appealing qualities a service leader has is the ability to engage and attract others who already think, or aspire to think, about life's bigger questions. The Mental : Intellectual dimension in your personal brand is a major leverage point you can use to attract others. We are often attracted to other people because of the quality of their ideas and thoughts. To go back to the Nashville point, especially in the music industry – which demands that each artist has his or her own signature sound – the quality of ideas, thoughts and mental energy can't be underestimated.

This is a slight departure from how Gad defines what he calls the mental dimension. He sees this dimension as one that can lead to personal transformation, which all great brands accomplish for their customers. The mental dimension lets brands affect people's lives by acting as agents or mental coaches who change how people think. Unlike the *Social : Relationship* dimension, which influences how much we feel we belong within our chosen groups, the *Mental : Intellectual* dimension influences how we integrate intellectually and ideologically within our groups. One of Gad's examples is from Volvo automobiles. As a group, Volvo owners may feel affinity towards one another, but the strength of the brand comes from how each vehicle promises to "satisfy an individual's need for security, comfort, and peace of mind."[5]

Turning back to your personal brand, some people are happy to not bother about high-minded things. This can put them at a disadvantage. Although this is a simplification, consider that early hunter-gatherers most likely only needed a good memory, relying on the wisdom and instruction from earlier generations for how to get food and what to do with the harvest. Compared with today's average person, our ancestors had significantly lower or less developed IQs.

In addition, someone with a small vocabulary is probably isolated from a lot of ideas. By itself a large vocabulary doesn't guarantee much, but to have a wide linguistic base you likely need to read a lot or regularly engage with people, which leads to being aware of many ideas. The chances are good that strong linguistic ability came from exposure to books and ideas, and broad exposure to the world beyond one's own existence enhances the *Mental : Intellectual* dimension. On the flipside, if you haven't been exposed to a wide variety of knowledge and don't have the vocabulary to effectively consider various topics or ideas, you won't be able to think on the level that will deliver the most valuable contribution to the group. I consider a true hallmark of intellectual prowess to be the ability to make connections between ideas in order to come up with newer and even better ones. Or, to put it another way, having strong intellectual ability is the ability to connect the dots and link ideas that aren't obvious or even intuitive.

By mental or intellectual I do not necessarily mean academic. There may be a case that people who have spent more time in school have been more exposed to ideas, but it's not necessarily true. Instead, a commitment to developing this dimension is the point. For example, a courier doesn't need much academic knowledge, but he or she needs to be able to troubleshoot and creatively problem solve. The ability to deal with new challenges and situations, balance common sense against the pros and cons of various alternatives, and each time pick the best solution for the issue at hand, is a sign that this person can think well on their feet. This independent thinking is what can lead to independent action. In a service setting, this mental ability helps the server fulfill the expectations and problem-solve the needs of even the most demanding clients.

Strengthening your *Mental : Intellectual* dimension can come by being a thoughtful, critical reader as well as a thoughtful, critical listener. I know many people I would call intellectual even though they don't read many books. Their source of knowledge is from their tribe.

Some people are generalists, Renaissance souls who want to be good at many things. This is opposed to the specialist, who dives into a topic to refine his/her understanding of a specific field or practice. The specialist will get the deeper meaning of things and the generalist will be better at connecting the dots across multiple subjects. The world is big enough to accommodate both types of people, but I expect the one with broader knowledge is the one who will be more innovative. In a service setting, problems are generally solved by bringing resources and ideas in new ways to design the best solution.

My friend Malcolm Au, who himself has been immensely successful as an entrepreneur and service leader, made the observation that I'm like a Chinese herbalist, and it's relevant to this discussion on the *Mental : Intellectual* dimension. Practitioners of Traditional Chinese Medicine, or TCM, are often supported by Chinese herbalists. These pharmacists often have shops with walls filled with cabinets and drawers that stocked all kinds of ingredients needed for prescriptions handed to patients by a TCM doctor. Traditionally, these herbalists would forage far and wide to collect branches, leaves, minerals, insects, animal parts and other ingredients. Then, once back at their shop, they would process the ingredients and store their collected samples in cabinets with their many drawers and cubby holes. A large part of the herbalist's skill was how he or she internalized and understood each ingredient for later use. Similarly, my pattern of thinking is to store and pull from ideas, insights and knowledge that I combine in various ways to create a solution to a tough challenge I need to fix. This kind of thinking is especially useful for problem solving, since it lets a person design solutions from across different domains and disciplines.

An example of why developing this dimension is crucial can be seen in how some men find it hard to work with or even talk to women. When it comes to personal service, this is a big disadvantage because it means this service provider is missing out on serving and learning from half the population. The ability to connect mentally and intellectually to all groups means you can connect with a wider pool of people, many who may think and act differently and on higher mental levels.

My hometown of Hong Kong has migrated from a manufacturing to a service economy, and the mentality has had to change to keep up. In the past, the city's people had the work ethic where putting in the hours was important; you worked long hours to complete production. In manufacturing, the people who stay on the line the longest are the most useful to the company. But in a service setting it's different. When you have a workplace where people need a strong *Mental : Intellectual* dimension, putting in the hours like a tireless machine is actually a liability. At their best, service providers have the mental energy to think on the fly and make the right decisions as conditions change. Today's Hong Kong is very different from our manufacturing-driven past. We're rightfully moving away from the ethic that demands long hours of physical labor towards a better, more mentally oriented, service-proficient workforce.

A study a few years ago explored workplace productivity across developed nations. Investigators found that whether people worked 40 hours or more than 70 hours a week, the average monthly productivity was about the same. One explanation is that in a service setting, mentally exhausted workers are less productive or less able to deliver the higher-value added tasks that service requires, so the total work output stays roughly constant. Value is linked to quantity under the manufacturing mindset, but this doesn't work as well in a service setting. Value in a service setting is linked to good character, since this means a person is less likely to repel others from making bad decisions.

When making an audit of your *Mental : Intellectual* dimension, take a moment to review (and measure, if you can) your productivity. To measure your productivity in loose terms that will be accurate enough for your purposes, keep a 'productivity' log that you update every week and keep some notes on what your energy and sleep levels are like. The chances are high that you will find that fatigue directly saps your own mental performance, and that when you're fresh you're at your most innovative. Also, part of this audit should also include an honest account of your own open-mindedness. Do you seek personal excellence from yourself and others from a vantage of intellectual humility? In other words, although you may expect a lot and demand the best from others, do you have the humility to be open-minded to all people and their ideas?

I'm a big believer in Liberal Arts education and that having a broad foundation can provide shortcuts on how to think and work better. This kind of educational exposure will let you sample ideas from across many disciplines, even if you only tap into it years after graduation. I also suggest memorizing the basics of whatever domain grabs your attention. In the book *Thinking, Fast and Slow*, by Daniel Kahneman, he discusses how many 1970s education theorists and practitioners rejected the role of memorization in childhood and later education.[15]

When Kahneman wrote his book, many believed rote memorization had something inherently wrong with it. In practice, though, rejecting memorization in learning isn't going to help you succeed in some things. For example, much as it's crucial that you understand why and how multiplication works in arithmetic, being able to multiply and divide works a lot better and faster if you simply memorize the multiplication tables.

When I studied fisheries management, a major part of getting the intellectual material down was to exercise critical thinking and have a conceptual understanding of why things were the way they were. However, basic information like fish anatomy, the different kinds of water bodies and predators of specific species simply had to be memorized. There wasn't any escaping that I needed to memorize the vocabulary and terms, but once the foundation was set, I could move on to tackle the harder and more conceptual material. Similarly, when I was with DHL, part of the mental development had to include the memorization of more than a hundred airport codes, be it HKG for Hong Kong, YYZ for Toronto, or LIM for Lima in Peru.

When it comes to how to strengthen and improve your *Mental : Intellectual* dimension, the best piece of advice is to commit to a path of lifelong learning, which is the subject of Chapter 15 on the *Lifelong Learning : Maturation* dimension. We see how important this is in the various professions – how accountants, doctors, lawyers and the rest have to get yearly CPD (continuous professional development) points. Apply that to your life and you will continuously upgrade your knowledge and skills to be a more competitive member of your tribe. Or, if you would like something more prescriptive, try to understand and practise the basics of as many different disciplines as you can. Yes, this will make you a 'Jack-of-all-trades', as the saying goes. But being this kind of generalist will inevitably mean you're therefore a 'master of none'. However, I don't think this is important because the mastery of service leadership almost demands that you be a Jack-of-all-trades, as this will give you as wide a scope of exposure to ideas as possible.

I will also add that all of this is not to diminish the importance of subconscious thinking. When driving a car, for example, beginners fumble because they have to consciously manage all the tasks and operations of driving and reading traffic. With so many things calling for the driver's conscious attention, making errors is part of the learning process. Over time and with practice, the skills and object awareness needed to be a competent driver are handled subconsciously, letting your conscious attention focus on higher-level issues.

Another way of thinking about this is that the *Mental : Intellectual* dimension is what helps you to make *better* decisions – not only make decisions. You can go through your day and not need to specifically use this dimension and survive perfectly well; arguably, on the production line this dimension is unnecessary. But if you're in service, and I believe everything above the production line is service, managing the strength of your *Mental : Intellectual* dimension should raise the bar for yourself and how you contribute to the group. Also, part of the practice of making better decisions requires that you can hold, consider, accept and reject many contradicting ideas. This contradiction is often a path to developing new ideas or finding new ways to find how to make better decisions.

If reading, studying or memorization doesn't fit your learning style, another good strategy is to find someone who can mentor you. This may not give you the detail you would get from studying the basics, but you can benefit from the person's experience and learn many shortcuts.

Returning to the Anna Karenina Principle, how this could bring someone down is that the expression of leadership can be through decision-making. A good leader is one who can inspire others behind his or her vision of where to go next, and an important part of that involves getting the correct information and paying attention to the right things. The examples abound of leaders with a big L and a little l, who failed with a big *F* and a little *f*, because they weren't able to get and use the right information when it mattered most. For yourself, just remember that keeping your *Mental : Intellectual* dimension strong is something you should be committed to throughout your life.

Connected to the Anna Karenina Principle is the notion of intellectual humility. Great service leaders must have the ability to think well and expansively, tempered with the humility to always allow for other, better ideas or new ways of thinking. This is also a good antidote to having the corrosive trait of hubris creep into the service leader's behavior - something that people will consistently avoid or find repellant. From Warren Buffett to Marie Curie, we see that truly great people are united with an intellectual humility that welcomes other ways of thinking, if only to widen one's mental horizons.

ACTION!

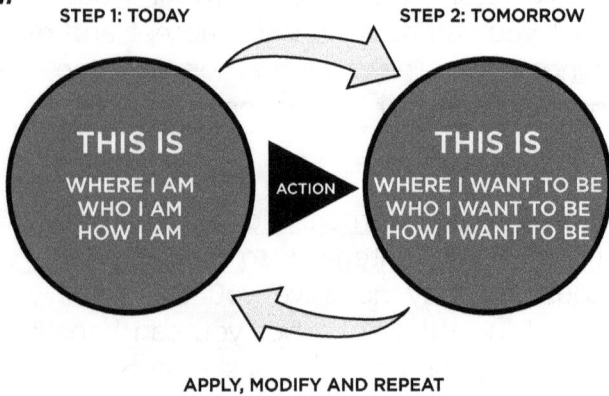

STEP 1: TODAY   STEP 2: TOMORROW

THIS IS
WHERE I AM
WHO I AM
HOW I AM

ACTION

THIS IS
WHERE I WANT TO BE
WHO I WANT TO BE
HOW I WANT TO BE

APPLY, MODIFY AND REPEAT

Review your *Mental : Intellectual* dimension and decide if it needs strengthening. This is the part of your personal brand that will greatly influence and enhance your ability to make decisions - the hallmark of a leader's activities. Make an honest review of this dimension and consider how to make changes that will become habit forming. Although this is mostly intellectual in spirit, it doesn't mean you need to change your learning style or dismiss how you think about things. It may simply involve broadening your appreciation for mental exploration, exercise, training and being more curious about the world.

Step 1: TODAY
Get a clear sense of your present situation. Write down the elements of your *Mental : Intellectual* dimension that affect where and how you live, work, and have fun in the different environments of your day-to-day world.

1. _____

2. _____

3. _____

4. _____

5. _____

Step 2: TOMORROW
Make an inventory of what you would like to be in the future. Although *Tomorrow* can literally mean tomorrow, it can also mean one or five years from now.

1. _____

2. _____

3. _____

4. _____

5. _____

Step 3: ACTION
Decide what you need to do to move from *Today* to *Tomorrow*. Define and carry out all actions, great and small, to

help move toward your goal.

1. _____

2. _____

3. _____

4. _____

5. _____

Step 4: APPLY, MODIFY, AND REPEAT

TOP CHEF IN ACTION – THE *MENTAL : INTELLECTUAL* DIMENSION

Sharon has a reputation for being a problem-solver, as a chef and as a businesswoman. During the first year of *Le Petit Plat*'s operation it was touch and go most of the time, even though they had a strong start. Luckily, she was part of an association of business owners that let her bounce ideas around and problem solve.

Sharon's *Mental : Intellectual* dimension is the kind that causes her to seek like-minded people who can meet her at her level. It's not that she's a bookworm or academic about where she gets inspired, but she's always reading the newspaper and trade magazines to stay up on trends in the industry, as well as getting insights on who's ahead and bringing innovation to the whole dining experience.

One month, it was her turn to host the business-owner's group she was a part of and she decided that in order to create a breakthrough for each business owner in their own business, she would team each business owner with someone from her staff so that her staff acted as masters to their new apprentices. This created some stressful situations in the kitchen and the dining room, as customers had to put up with mistakes and poor service delivery from inside the kitchen and in the dining room.

It was a big risk, but Sharon knew that the experience would teach each business owner something new about the service-delivery process, maybe even change how each person thought about how they delivered service in their own business.

Although she went out on a limb, what her peers had learned was an invaluable lesson from the trenches about service.

Chapter
ELEVEN

The *Spiritual : Inspirational* Dimension

Chapter Summary:
This dimension is deeply personal and delicate. Rather than being a podium you use to recruit others, this contains the motives behind your actions that address issues greater than you – this is what will last after your entrepreneurial journey has come to an end.

Discussing this dimension is delicate. It is a subjective, personal dimension for all of us, even for those who would argue against the idea of a 'spiritual' self. By your *Spiritual : Inspirational* dimension, I don't only mean your religious beliefs and commitment to a chosen faith, although that is certainly a significant influence in many people's lives. Instead, this is what connects you to the outside world, and how you can help others connect to things that are bigger than all of us. This dimension can refer to religion, commitment to the environment, or anything outside your immediate world.

Anyone living a reflective life will sooner or later ask, *why am I here? Can I contribute to something bigger than what's right in front of me?* Returning to Gad, he called the spiritual dimension of a brand what refers to the bigger set of systems that we are a part of. The reason it's crucial that we review our own *Spiritual : Inspirational* dimension is because, as Gad wrote, "understand the spiritual and you understand the connections between the brand, the product or the company, and the bigger system."

From within your personal brand, this means you will understand the connection between yourself and everyone else, and to the greater systems around you. Gad described how The Body Shop transcended simple body-care products and created a brand that fulfilled the functional, emotional, mental and spiritual needs of its consumers. This is very powerful, and if dealt with maturely and with sensitivity, it can separate you as a service leader with relevance and deep connection.

Given the thorniness of the subject and that there is a spectrum out there ranging from the highly orthodox to the vocally atheist, I suspect that for this dimension, either you feel a sense of faith or you don't. However, it's a part of you that others may be interested in, so it's in your interest to know what's important to you and what's guiding you, if anything at all.

In my case, I've had times when I felt there was something off or incomplete in my life in the traditional sense, a feeling sometimes called 'spiritual'. Philosophies and guiding principles I've explored came from Buddhism, Confucianism and Taoism. I've also explored Christianity, but it didn't lead to the closure that I expected would come with deep religious connection. After being a successful businessman, I retired and explored one of my earlier passions, natural science.

Again, this dimension can be touchy, in that someone could read this and think I'm lost, seeking some kind of redemption, or whatever else. However, given that this is all deeply personal, I invite you not to jump to conclusions about my own dimension, but simply to join me without judgment and hear me out – if it makes sense, great. If it doesn't, that's also great. The point being that for a long time I explored the territory of what is traditionally called spiritual and have since found my own personal route to what satisfies my *Spiritual : Inspirational* dimension.

One way to get a constructive overview of what falls under this dimension is to survey what's out there and go with what speaks to you. To start, you may want to explore the lessons found in the tradition you were born into. In my case, I was born into the Buddhist, Confucian and Taoist traditions, as well as the Christian tradition. As I've matured, I have kept what works for me and left the rest. Also, when I was younger, I didn't have a need for any of these things, but have increasingly turned to them with the passing years.

When it comes to your personal brand, you will enhance how others perceive you when they see that you are committed to concerns beyond yourself. That you also tackle interests that relate to the greater good. To audit and address your own dimension, I suggest that after you've learned about the tradition you were born into, give the other traditions a review. You can include the various schools of philosophy and social causes that tackle issues that go beyond material needs. See if you find anything in there that motivates you or sit with someone considered a leader in your community to see if he or she can share something that speaks to you. In essence, stay curious and take the time to get your metaphysical feet wet.

Some would argue that the deep insights that reveal truths only come from deep and concentrated study, and this comes from committing to a religious or spiritual tradition. This may be true, but I would add that this part of your journey is like learning an instrument. If you aren't drawn to any one in particular, be it a guitar or piano or drums, try your hand at all of them and see which one resonates most with who you are. Follow your heart. If you're a seeker, there's something out there that will fulfill your *Spiritual : Inspirational* dimension. If not, no need to beat yourself up about it – maybe this just isn't something you need. For myself, my own spiritual journey was informed by what I learned in university, when I studied fisheries management. I learned to think of the fish, then the school of fish, and then the ecosystem. I connected these to Buddhism, Confucianism and Taoism, respectively.

Politics, for its part, can be included, but isn't completely part of this dimension. Although political movements can inform and even drastically influence personal, national and international policies and behaviors, it's not a perfect fit. The *Spiritual : Inspirational* dimension is the part of you that you can imagine to last beyond you when you're no longer alive. It's also what tackles issues that are of almost historical importance from the prism of your life.

Why this matters to you as a service provider is because there may be people in your life who are looking for help and this is one way to support them. I suggest treading lightly when going out to help people on this, as it's doubtful anyone needs 'help' with their *Spiritual : Inspirational* dimension, unless they ask for it. Like discussing politics, it may be more productive to let people in your team be the source of the questions and you can focus on being a source of inspiration.

This dimension is something that may drive and direct how some people choose to live and manage their activities, but for many, like me, it took until retirement before I discovered what my spiritual self actually needed. While I was with DHL, I can't say spiritual concerns mattered much, but when I started preparing my departure I began to appreciate what the greater good was. I began to appreciate the metaphysical contribution I made by helping people around the world carry out their international trade. I helped make international trade work better and faster, which for me was deeply moving. I mentioned this to my colleagues, and then it became a conscious appreciation of what we were doing. This had great spiritual and motivational power across our offices.

ACTION!

STEP 1: TODAY   STEP 2: TOMORROW

THIS IS

WHERE I AM
WHO I AM
HOW I AM

ACTION

THIS IS

WHERE I WANT TO BE
WHO I WANT TO BE
HOW I WANT TO BE

APPLY, MODIFY AND REPEAT

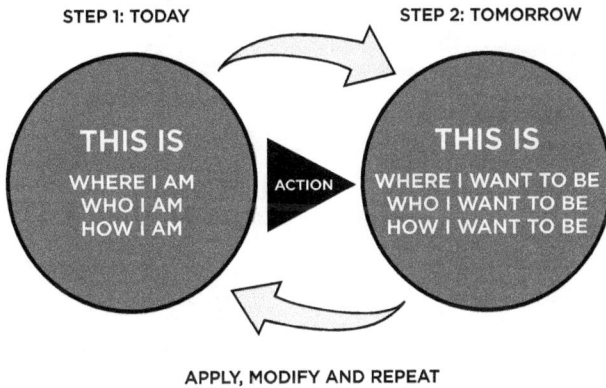

Review your *Spiritual : Inspirational* dimension and decide if it needs strengthening. This is the part of your personal brand that can inspire others to great loyalty because it communicates why you work and what you expect your contribution to mean. Make an honest review of your dimension and consider making some changes. For this dimension, remember that it's about contributing to what is bigger than you and your immediate needs for the greater good. In a way, this is service leadership at its highest ideal. Nevertheless, what drives you could be a passion rooted in your faith, in helping the needy, or it could be in helping to protect the environment. Ultimately, clarifying for yourself what the content of this dimension is for you and understanding how to strengthen it is sure to inspire those in your life on a deep and personally fulfilling level.

Step 1: TODAY
Get a clear sense of your present situation. Write down the elements of your *Spiritual : Inspirational* dimension that affect where and how you live, work, and have fun in the different environments of your day-to-day world.

1. _____

2. _____

3. _____

4. _____

5. _____

Step 2: TOMORROW
Make an inventory of what you would like to be in the future. Although *Tomorrow* can literally mean tomorrow, it can also mean one or five years from now.

1. _____

2. _____

3. _____

4. _____

5. _____

Step 3: ACTION
Decide what you need to do to move from *Today* to *Tomorrow*. Define and carry out all actions, great and small, to

help move toward your goal.

1. _____

2. _____

3. _____

4. _____

5. _____

Step 4: APPLY, MODIFY, AND REPEAT

TOP CHEF IN ACTION - THE *SPIRITUAL : INSPIRATIONAL* DIMENSION

Le Petit Plat promises one of the finest dining experiences in the city. Every detail around the restaurant points to the mission of being one of the best French restaurants in town. Although this has been Sharon's main goal, she understands that her restaurant ultimately isn't about making nice food for people.

By apprenticing in Paris and getting submerged in the culture of French cooking, Sharon understood she was representing a culinary history that went back hundreds of years and would likely remain a dominant culinary force. Added to this was that Sharon was committed to making the *Le Petit Plat* a community partner, focused on being profitable as to making an impact in the lives of people in the community.

Every quarter, the restaurant would host cooking classes for the city's underprivileged youth, showing a way to improve their lives by eating well and even embarking on a path of cooking. After nearly a year of such classes, Sharon built a reputation as a business owner and leader who is also committed to improving the lives around her.

For her staff, she regularly invites guest chefs to come and show techniques and other trade information. As an added bonus, she launched a merit program to reward the people who go the extra mile. Rather than giving a financial bonus, employees receive one-on-one training in the subject of their choice, even if it doesn't have anything to do with the restaurant business.

Chapter
TWELVE

The *Physical : Health* Dimension

Chapter Summary:
This dimension involves your physical health, supported by balanced living habits that optimize your ability to maintain high stamina.

When your health is good you may not notice it, but when you're sick it can directly impact your quality of life. Being and feeling fit and healthy isn't necessarily noticed, but being unfit and unhealthy can completely take over your life. Clearly, your *Physical : Health* dimension has to at least be stable if not vibrant in order for you to succeed. Yet there are many inspiring cases when the truly dedicated and committed pushed through significant pain or physical hardship to achieve greatness. Among sports athletes, we can look at the now infamous Lance Armstrong, the Tour de France champion cyclist who overcame cancer to win (and then get stripped of) seven race titles. A more inspiring example would be renowned astrophysicist Stephen Hawking, who has battled motor neuron disease throughout his life, leaving him almost entirely paralyzed. Yet, he helped significantly expand the whole domain of physics. These very different examples can be assessed by how strong these people are in their other 11 dimensions, but for now the focus remains on their *Physical : Health* dimension.

Auditing this dimension is important because without a stable level of health, we won't get much done – a lack of health creates a significant barrier to being productive. As we age, we increasingly find our health deteriorating, but for decades we can expect a level of health that will sustain us. Unless we do something to corrupt it (such as substance abuse) or an external source threatens our health (such as a disease), most of us can expect our bodies to run fairly well.

We should review and enhance our *Physical : Health* dimension because it will help us maintain our stamina and energy, the kind that lets us stay alert and capable. If we're sickly or frail, although most people won't explicitly stay away from us, they may begin avoiding us, especially if we're perceived as a threat to their health. The most acute warning sign to others is if we have or are thought to have a communicable disease. Another stark example is if you have some kind of rare disease; people may stay away out of ignorance because they fear catching what you have.

Service leadership isn't about finding the quickest route to solve a problem or how to find shortcuts. If there's a common trait to the world's best service leaders, it's that their success was built on hard and deep work, the kind of physical and mental effort that demands our best.[16] There are habits and practices that can support our peak performance and much of it relates to our *Physical : Health* dimension. This is the kind of foundation that lets everything else shine.

Keeping optimal health can be extremely complex, but for managing what you can control, a good place to start is to try to maintain a bright, optimistic personality and outlook on life, supported by healthy living habits. All else being equal, you will probably have an easier time attracting others if your approach to life and personal brand are known to be constructive and positive. Another critical factor is to maintain a good level of exercise, especially when you have the kinds of expectations, deliverables and schedule that people at the top have to deal with. Your diet is important and you need the discipline to know when to draw the line at what you will and will not put into your body.

We probably aren't that different from our ancestors who lived tens of thousands of years ago. Although human culture has developed and is still evolving at a dizzying pace, we are biologically bound by limits on how much our bodies can change. Convincing evidence suggests that our bodies take hundreds of thousands of years to change, and between now and, say, 50,000 years ago, our bodies have mostly stayed the same as those of our ancestors. On that alone, it would make sense to understand what people ate and did in the past. Therefore, given that our ancestors were hunter-gatherers, we should stick to that kind of diet – one that is low on meat and high on grains, fruit, and vegetables. If you find that your diet needs attention, you can benefit by following a good diet through the aid of a menu planner. There are home-catering and dietician services that will send you monthly diets and recipes to follow. In some areas, for a few dollars a month, you can even get your meals delivered by someone who will do the menu planning for you.

To start, consider understanding what your *Physical : Health* dimension needs, seeing how it is perceived by others, and where you may want to improve it. If you're seen within your tribe as a consistently healthy and vibrant person, this will appeal to others and draw them to you. On the other hand, if you're always seen as down or sick, the danger is that it will take over your personal brand and you will be disadvantaged by people's perception of the limited value you bring to your group.

Having a weak dimension can compromise your personal

brand, but having a strong dimension may not affect your personal brand at all. The chances are your health will probably go under the radar. If you have a weak Physical : Health dimension, you have a strong reason to find strategies to improve or strengthen it.

I have a friend who has raced in many of the grueling Iron Man triathlons and he is more than 65 years old. It doesn't take long for people to notice that he's a guy with impressive stamina and resilience. In fact, it is such a part of who he is that his personal brand and image are statements about his being an Iron Man. It's not that he's always bringing it up, but being an Iron Man is just what naturally comes across through his actions, words and deeds.

In service leadership, someone with a strong, vibrant Physical : Health dimension is going to communicate to others that he or she is competent and up to the challenge. Not only that, people who have a vibrant energy communicate to others that they are physically up to the challenges of leadership – an attractive force when people want to follow someone they can trust to be around for a while.

Also, a person's dimension will most likely have an effect if it's on the negative side, not the positive. A service leader prone to being sick will probably not succeed as well as someone who is healthy, although it will probably go unnoticed if this person's health is on the healthier end of the spectrum.

An element of one's Physical : Health dimension that will always enhance one's personal brand is the perception of one's stamina. Tireless people who push through even when things are tough have an attractive and admirable personal brand. Stamina includes the grit and determination to manage the stresses of life. We must all manage increasingly complex tasks and deadlines, many of which could push us to breaking point. For many, stress can manifest in our bodies, eventually destabilizing our health (for example, it's common to have stress-related bowel or skin ailments). When reviewing your dimension, it helps to get an accurate assessment of your health and find the best strategy for ensuring you're able to stay in the game until the end. In fact, if you happen to have an especially stressful job, like a broker or other time-sensitive career, you should be even more diligent about this dimension.

Remember that we tend to be drawn to other's energy and the energetic people in our groups. If you're someone who can't energize the people around you, the chances are that you won't be able to get your team to deliver as much or as quickly as other high-performers out there. For any role that requires leadership by action, maintaining a high energy level is crucial. This may be bound by your personal temperament, but even people who are completely laid back can kick it into gear when the situation demands it.

Dedication to one's *Physical : Health* dimension is fundamental and necessary. It doesn't matter if it's dance, martial arts or triathlons, this is an essential dimension that shouldn't be overlooked or neglected. Looking at it through the lens of the Anna Karenina Principle, a review of your dimension could lead you to make that tough decision to quit smoking, drinking to excess, eating poorly, not exercising, or doing all those things that could eventually make you sick or stop you in your tracks.

ACTION!

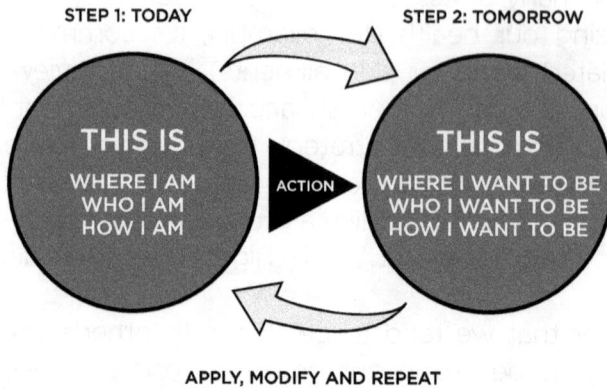

STEP 1: TODAY   STEP 2: TOMORROW

THIS IS   **THIS IS**

WHERE I AM   ACTION   WHERE I WANT TO BE
WHO I AM   WHO I WANT TO BE
HOW I AM   HOW I WANT TO BE

APPLY, MODIFY AND REPEAT

Review your *Physical : Health* dimension and decide if it needs strengthening. This is the part of your personal brand that most affects your stamina and ability to deliver. If it's weak it can lead people to avoid you. Make an honest review of this dimension and consider making some changes. For example, are you maintaining a regular sleep cycle? This may sound trivial, but the truly successful have long been advocates of getting enough sleep. An exhausted service leader won't be in the best state to rise to the occasions of service leadership. Make an honest appraisal of your *Physical : Health* dimension in order to cover how well this dimension is working for you.

Step 1: TODAY
Get a clear sense of your present situation. Write down the elements of your *Physical : Health* dimension that affect your health and physical state. This includes fitness level, sleep and eating habits, if and how well you keep your environment right to support a healthy lifestyle, and all the qualities that you would like to change.

1. _____

2. _____

3. _____

4. _____

5. _____

Step 2: TOMORROW
Make an inventory of what you would like to be in the future.
Although *Tomorrow* can literally mean tomorrow, it can also mean one or five years from now.

1. _____

2. _____

3. _____

4. _____

5. _____

Step 3: ACTION
Decide what you need to do to move from *Today* to *Tomorrow*. Define and carry out all actions great and small to help move toward your goal.

1. _____

2. _____

3. _____

4. _____

5. _____

Step 4: APPLY, MODIFY, AND REPEAT

TOP-CHEF IN ACTION – THE *PHYSICAL : HEALTH* DIMENSION

Ever since she was in cooking school, Sharon was a passionate cyclist. At *Le Petit Plat*, she would always ride to and from the restaurant on her bike, as her house was a good hour's ride away. Sharon was as passionate about exercise as she was about everything else in her life. She would commute to the restaurant by bike, rain or shine, and she encouraged all her staff to do the same. She understood that in order to maintain her stamina as a chef, she needed to maintain her overall physical fitness and health.

This commitment was not only how she behaved outside of the restaurant, but also in the menu choices she created. The ingredients had to be excellent and she was committed to having a healthy relationship to the food she would serve to customers. She could not feel that her service to her customers and staff was the best that it could be if she cut corners around the ingredients she chose or the dishes she served.

Within her team, her commitment to living a healthy life was a model to everyone else, to the point that over time her staff began to follow her example. The message she tried to communicate was that she was an active part of Le Petit Plat's work engine – that her energy was shared and amplified by all her staff, and this was reflected in the food. From the quality ingredients to the perfectly-portioned and designed plates, the consistent message was that Le Petit Plat was a restaurant that delivered healthy food from balanced start to decadent finish.

Chapter THIRTEEN

The *Economic : Security* Dimension

Chapter Summary:
This dimension demands an honest review of what you need, what you want, where you are, and where you want to be. Managing this dimension means clearly understanding what your temptations are, where greed could take over, and how to put on the brakes when you need them.

Most of us have felt at some time in our lives the stress of not having enough resources and the limits this can have on what we are able to do. For too many, the pressures of their *Economic : Security* dimension can be a debilitating source of frustration, fear and pain. As with the other dimensions, you would do well to find the right balance that works for you so that you can take care of all 12 of them. If building wealth is your dominant goal and a powerful driver, consider setting a benchmark you can live with or would like to have. Once you hit it, you can ease off the throttle and start looking at other areas in your life. There are many whose motivation for accumulating money is to avoid suffering now and in the future, and this is a valid concern for your survival. The danger is losing perspective and making this dimension your most important one.

A good way of understanding the *Economic : Security* dimension is to consider its opposite, the toxic reverse that harms instead of helps your financial health over the long term. For this dimension, the toxic reverse is jealousy or greed. Much of having a stable dimension is managing your expectations of what you need to feel stable, and for the *Economic : Security* dimension this means reviewing what wealth and security means to you, and how much is enough to bring you the financial freedom you want. For some, always wanting more or expecting too much can leave them unhappy or bitter, because realization of an unrealistic dream is a nightmare that keeps stretching away from them. Although many people are wealthy in relative terms and have more than enough to comfortably survive, they see what they have as never enough and fail to reach feelings of satisfaction or peace.

Since we can't manage what we can't see, for the *Economic : Security* dimension I suggest keeping a log of your earnings and spending. A personal balance sheet of your finances will put specific values in front of you that you can use for reference and planning. This is a great way to see how you're spending and saving your income, week to week. The impact of this dimension on others comes when you don't have a basic amount of money to cover your needs and you suffer for it. Then, the people around you may worry about your security; that from desperation you will make bad choices or go after dead ends, or that you will target others to skim their assets for yourself.

You can review and strengthen your *Economic : Security* dimension with the help of a good financial advisor. By financial advisor, I don't mean someone who manages your money with investments. Instead, a real financial advisor is someone who gives you the knowledge, skills and financial intelligence that most people don't get. One good way to check if a financial advisor is right for you is to find out if their income is aligned with your profit. Avoid situations where your wealth increases through natural growth but your advisor makes money on commissions from trading with your cash. That conflict of interest will pull your advisor towards more trading (how he or she makes their money), and not on creating actual growth from your investments. In other words, avoid listening to anyone whose interest isn't directly aligned with yours.

One economic shortcut is to leverage the power of compound interest. There are many resources available that explain how to leverage compound interest, so I will detail a few key points. The quick answer is that it's interest on your investment that earns you more interest. For example, suppose you saved $100 one year ago and it earned $2 in interest from the bank over that year. The next year, you will earn interest on your original $100 plus the $2 interest you earned. It may seem like nothing, but compound interest can have profound effects on your savings. This principle was most famously described by Albert Einstein, who wrote, "Compound interest is the eighth wonder of the world. He who understands it, earns it ... He who doesn't ... Pays it." If you have credit card bills piling up and you notice that no matter how much you pay your bills the total still isn't going down, you're on the losing end of the compound interest equation. Better to be on the savings end and watch your capital grow exponentially. If you have credit cards, make sure you pay off the full balance each and every month.

Another shortcut is to cut costs and save the difference for another day. This is one of the least flashy yet most underrated wealth creators at anyone's disposal.

From your *Economic : Security* dimension comes the mindset that manages your wealth – no matter how large or small. Wealth management is scalable, so even if your income is small you can still apply the same principles of financial management that you would find among the wealthy, and hopefully in your more prosperous future. You must be persistent, honest and disciplined about understanding your drives and behaviors. This mindful persistence or conscientiousness is the hallmark of the truly successful. Part of this means you need to review this dimension in your personal brand to see what works and what doesn't.

For example, do you have the integrity and honesty to admit to yourself if you're being greedy? Or, just as importantly, do you have the strength to walk away if one of your close friends or associates is trying to sell you on a deal that will leave you disadvantaged? The nuance here is that there's a fine line separating greed from ambition. For starters, having an ambition and being ambitious is separated by temperament, where being ambitious can be aggressive and can repel others. Again looking at Lance Armstrong, he probably began with the ambition to be the world's greatest cyclist. Then, after being corrupted by the toxic qualities of his win-at-all-costs ambition for so long, his toxic behavior resulted in a dramatic fall from grace that left him banned from the sport and stripped of his titles.

Similarly, greed is ambition focused on the goal of building wealth at all costs. Greed is about winner-take-all and it's hard to feel satisfied with what's in the bank. It's safe to say that almost everyone wants to get rich, yet it's highly likely that the greed on Wall Street is more naked and explicit than what we find in other places.

An audit of this dimension should include ways to decrease the potential of greed getting the best of you. Where ambition sets a goal you aim to reach, greed will move the goalpost each time because you want more, more, more.

I don't mean to suggest that there's something wrong with

having a lot of money. Given my success after retiring from DHL, that would be disingenuous. However, if wealth alone is your driver, the chances are that you won't find it fulfilling once you reach it. For example, most entrepreneurs I've met aren't ever satisfied; that's the fire in their bellies that keeps them pushing their start-ups from failure to success. However, for the truly successful entrepreneurs out there, the fire in the belly isn't to make money but to use a business to solve a pain that helps people.

If we look at this dimension through the filter of the service provider, it's easy to see how a wealth-driven model of service falls apart. Service-centered companies that are revenue or profit driven must be careful to ensure that profit-making goals never step on the toes of the people who receive the service. To put it another way, a service company that puts profit above delighting its clients will eventually find that client loyalty will only go as far as the current invoice. Once the competition offers a discounted rate, clients will jump.

In managing your *Economic : Security* dimension, I suggest you orient your moneymaking to activities that aren't toxic or viral. First, raise your standards and set a bottom line that you will not cross, then stick to it or find ways to protect yourself from giving in to temptations that can come with success. This arrogance or hubris that comes with success can blind you to the corrupted service you are providing, and this is a common example of how the Anna Karenina Principle can bring down a service leader.

One trait I've consistently found among truly successful business leaders is that they are humble. They have both intellectual and leadership humility, recognizing that their position is based on respect and trust that they won't dare taint with arrogance or hubris. They work harder than everyone else in their company and don't let their success go to their head. Conversely, the wannabes and leaders with a small 'I' are the least humble and most toxic. This hubris shows up in many ways, from being rude with junior staff to being unappreciative of a client's conditions and pains. There are few things less toxic in a service moment than one party taking the other for granted. Another way of putting this is to remember and respect that your ideas are not necessarily the best. Although unlikely, it's possible that a service leader could even consistently come up with bad ideas, as long as he or she can then choose the better ideas coming from the team.

It's even more important to keep your integrity when times are tough than when things are going well. When there are no temptations and everything is great, sticking to the default of being good and true to your word is easy. It takes little energy to steer a ship moving with the current in the right direction. On the other hand, it's much harder to do the right thing when you're surrounded by temptation and moving against the tides.

At one point, I held 100% of DHL International Ltd.'s shares, when I was only entitled to the Asia Pacific territory. I could have kept it that way and not honored the promises and guarantees I had made to my team as we grew. Although the wealth that I could have kept could have been massive, I simply had to honor my promises and be true to my word. It was the right thing to do, since not to have done so would have destroyed the trust we had built. Adding those kinds of toxic behaviors and viruses into the network could have even dragged whole network into serious trouble. I would have created a real mess if I wasn't true to my word – legal, personal, financial and much more.

If being wealthy is too far off on the horizon, I suggest first aiming for financial independence. They're both liberating. Having independence will bring you peace of mind, as much as if you had millions in the bank. The peace of mind of not stressing every day to make ends meet and not having debts looming over your head will leave you a lot more energy to focus on your other dimensions and the things you really love.

ACTION!

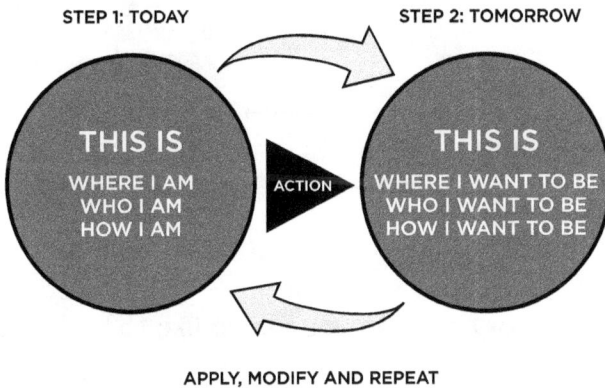

STEP 1: TODAY

STEP 2: TOMORROW

THIS IS
WHERE I AM
WHO I AM
HOW I AM

ACTION

THIS IS
WHERE I WANT TO BE
WHO I WANT TO BE
HOW I WANT TO BE

APPLY, MODIFY AND REPEAT

Review your *Economic : Security* dimension and decide if it needs strengthening. This is the part of your personal brand that can sharply raise your anxiety, which can impact your ability to deliver great personal service. Make an honest review of your dimension and consider making some changes. For this dimension, you may need to revise how you feel about deeply personal things like your ideas of financial security, success and wealth. There is tremendous advantage in learning from others, be it through conversations or books. There are many resources out there to help you get a stronger *Economic : Security* dimension.

Step 1: TODAY
Get a clear sense of your present situation. Write down the elements of your *Economic : Security* dimension that affect where and how you live, work, and have fun in the different

environments of your day-to-day world. This includes your financial profile, expenses and income, your debts, and all the details that relate to your financial profile.

1. _____

2. _____

3. _____

4. _____

5. _____

Step 2: TOMORROW
Make an inventory of what you would like to be in the future. Although *Tomorrow* can literally mean tomorrow, it can also mean one or five years from now.

1. _____

2. _____

3. _____

4. _____

5. _____

Step 3: ACTION
Decide what you need to do to move from *Today* to *Tomorrow*. Define and carry out all actions, great and small, to help move toward your goal.

1. _____

2. _____

3. _____

4. _____

5. _____

Step 4: APPLY, MODIFY AND REPEAT

TOP CHEF IN ACTION – THE *ECONOMIC : SECURITY* DIMENSION

Now approaching the third year of operation, *Le Petit Plat*'s founder and key staff are reviewing the restaurant's financial health. For the first year, Sharon went most months without taking a salary. With two solid years behind them, Sharon is now considering a financial review.

One reason the restaurant has done so well is because there is a clear separation of what it takes to make fine food and what it takes to run a sustainable, profitable business. As a chef, she holds to principles of using the best ingredients, preparing them with the utmost finesse, and composing dishes that are balanced and refined. As a business owner, she holds to the principles of paying more to hire and keep the best people, and structuring the business to deliver the highest value to customers while still achieving large profit margins.

Before launching the restaurant, Sharon sought help from a business consultant. Together, they defined the financial milestones, costs and other business metrics so that *Le Petit*

Plat was as financially stable as could be expected. This exercise was critical for Sharon to know what she needed to do for the restaurant to run efficiently and profitably. Even in a downturn, the restaurant could still fulfill its promise to all suppliers and staff – including herself. Ultimately, no one's *Economic : Security* dimension would be threatened.

Chapter
FOURTEEN

The *Leader : Follower* Dimension

Chapter Summary:
Your ability to grow and succeed as a leader is the degree to which you have developed your Competence, Character and Care. The blend of the three represents your leadership potential, and as you build all areas, be aware that even minor faults in one dimension can end up costing you all your credibility and trustworthiness. As a shortcut to enhancing this dimension, be sure to explore opportunities to find people who can be your master or apprentice.

What is a leader? This little question is stubbornly hard to answer. I've had many discussions on the topic, and the best definition I've found is that a leader is someone who has followers. Without followers, that 'leader' is just somebody taking a walk. Today, and this is especially true with service leaders, a leader's success depends on how well he or she influences others that they couldn't otherwise control without money or force. This could also be called one's personal soft power.

While I was heading DHL's Asia Pacific operation, I had to exercise what I thought was the right way to lead our teams. This was a practice of leading in the trenches, day in and day out. Since leaving DHL and getting introspective about my experience, I've spent a lot of time exploring and refining what's needed to make a great leader for a service team of followers. These weren't just anyone who happened to be there, but a team of followers who themselves worked under the highest competence, character and care. I understood that money was enough to get competent followers, and if money wasn't enough then status or power would do the trick. The issue was that for building the most competitive group of service leaders, I couldn't attract and retain people with character and care if I didn't have character and care myself.

The reason I'm convinced we all have a *Leader : Follower* dimension is because we are moving into the Service Age. When manufacturing was dominant, leaders commanded and controlled from the top of the hierarchy or organizational pyramid. They made decisions and the people down the pyramid did what they were told. In the Service Age, everyone must be able to inspire and engage one-another to make the right decision given a particular situation. Whereas leadership in manufacturing is about decision-making to improve quality by designing consistent and repeated production of things, leadership in service is about decision-making between people when variability and complexity are always possible.

Leadership in service is less of a pyramid shape and more like a scaffold held together with trust and respect. At any given moment, unique pressures and situations crop up that demand local leadership and decision-making. When crises develop or the inevitable twist comes up, everyone across the organization can act at the local level to solve problems on-site. Moreover, the level of trustworthiness a person has will directly influence on how well he or she is perceived. This is what empowers people to be autonomous leaders and this is what helps a service team be more competitive.

Before the production line was invented and industrialization took over a few hundred years ago, leadership was mostly a service-oriented practice for getting things done. For example, kings were in the business of providing services to their people, religious leaders as well, and blacksmiths and other tradesmen were also service providers. This all changed with industrialization and mass manufacturing.

I have heard many students say that they have no interest in leadership or that promotion isn't the shared goal of the masses. What I have answered is that although the idea of leadership may not be attractive, almost every parent realizes that once you have to be the guardian for another person, you directly experience what it means to be a leader who serves. As parents, we must provide leadership to our children because they are always looking to see how we act and react. Often, they judge us across our 12 dimensions – even if it isn't conscious. Also, even siblings share the role of leading one another.

If you aren't a leader in your current job, you'd best believe that if you start a family you will be promoted up your tribe to lead your small family. One way of looking at the family – and this might seem brutal but it's still worth considering – is that they are all small tribal units trying to out-compete the rest and prove better equipped for survival.

This dimension has been the subject of many books and training programs. Leadership is subdivided into its functional parts – including communication, caring, empathy, educational training, and addressing your EQ. I believe the best path to success in strengthening this dimension is by refining your other dimensions. For example, although your *Leader : Follower* dimension may not enhance your *Visual : Daily* Management dimension, the latter dimension will certainly influence how you are perceived as a leader.

Leadership is truly a service we deliver to others, established on the trustworthiness we inspire. This dimension is critical when we have the opportunity to provide others with support, guidance or information. Over time, we will see that people will barter with us in order to get that extra bit of service from you. Of the 12 dimensions, the *Leader : Follower* and *Competence : Expertise* dimensions are the two that will prompt most people to look to us for active contribution.

As I mentioned in Chapter 3, the key ingredients behind a great service leader are his or her 3-Cs of Competence, Character and Care. By making each one as strong as possible, the intersection of the 3-Cs is our leadership potential. This is also the building block for establishing and maintaining our level of trustworthiness.

Many people aspire to develop their leadership dimension because they're aiming to be the top-of-the-hierarchy leader, which is likely due to the seductive temptations of power. Putting that aside, one key to the practice of leadership comes from a Zen or Taoist approach, where a strong moral compass and doing what's right will let us become good leaders. Otherwise, we could end up leading everyone in the wrong direction.

In countries where leadership is concentrated and where corruption seems to be more of an institutional problem, the 12 Dimensions model suggests that a holistic, balanced leadership is missing. The result is that strategic plans don't look far enough and the people at the top are probably light on trustworthiness. Then there's the issue of what is the country's vision to inspire its people forward – is the vision one the nation will follow, let alone everyone around the world? We see that as countries increasingly let information flow, people follow. Given the choice, people will choose to follow the leaders they trust and the vision that goes beyond the self-serving interest of the ruling party.

This is all very 'grand' – very epic in proportion. Let's also narrow things a bit and look at the tribe of the classroom, an environment where someone wants to emerge as a leader. Again, this leadership is a service you would be delivering to fellow students through a healthy blend of Competence, Character and Care. In exercising these over time, the classmates will reinforce their acceptance and trust, which builds self-esteem in the leader. Self-esteem is vital because it's a reinforcing loop – the more you have, the greater your confidence, and this confidence will let you build on your service success, giving you greater self-esteem and everything that follows from that.

Like a balloon in your chest, self-esteem can swell or get squeezed by the pressures around you. As an important part of your self-image, having a healthy and not over-inflated self-esteem ensures you can make tough decisions and stick to them, especially if you run into resistance from within or beyond the group.

The resilience and depth of a person's self-esteem mostly comes from making mistakes and not falling into the trap of self-doubt, or worse. As Winston Churchill suggested, "Success is moving from mistake to mistake without losing enthusiasm."

One of the conscious things my wife, Helen, and I did with our three daughters was to help them build self-esteem through responsibilities of increasingly greater importance. Because of their successes and failures, they've emerged with healthy self-esteem and are leaders in their respective personal and professional worlds. Looking at DHL, we helped our couriers by empowering them and making them responsible at street level, building up their self-esteem to make decisions and take things into their own hands.

One way to build up the stamina of your self-esteem is to chunk it down by making small decisions every day that will boost your momentum. Rather than aiming for the top, potentially falling short and losing enthusiasm or momentum, aim a little lower. Still give it some real effort, but make the goal close enough to let you consistently reach it and feel the rush of achievement. Like with the 'flow' state discussed in Chapter 9, if you make your goal too easy it won't give you as much of a boost, but when the goal is just challenging enough and you hit a bunch of goals every day, eventually you'll find that your leadership muscles are strong.

One rebuttal of all this could be that everyone can't lead all the time. A team made up of leaders won't get far. Although this is generally true if the mindset is that of the leader at the top of the pyramid, it isn't true if the model we use is that of a scaffold. Once it's a seamless network of connected leaders who can act at the local level as needed, then everyone can be a leader at the same time. This scaffold is the structure of service leadership.

I suggest that if your leadership dimension isn't fully developed and you're not in an environment that will let you step forward, at least work on developing your Competence, Character and Care, because sooner or later the time will come when you will have to lead.

I sometimes get a student who asks me, *what if the aspiration to be a leader is missing?* I don't argue back; the excuse is a bit of a cop-out that reveals more about how the student feels about themselves and their own levels of self-esteem. The fact is that whether we like and seek out leadership roles or not, we are all faced with moments in our relationships when we are called upon to lead. If we don't step in to fill that vacuum, someone else will do it for us. Ultimately, not filling in those moments to show some leadership is a recipe for stagnation and it could mean never seeing a promotion.

Becoming a better leader means developing one's *Leader: Follower* dimension and for that to happen we must be self-aware. By being aware of the importance, ingredients and paths to leadership, and committed to improving, this awareness followed up with action is a great recipe for success.

On the opposite side, a recipe for disaster is to let the Anna Karenina Principle work under the radar, only to ultimately bring us to failure. Leadership is about ensuring that all 12 dimensions are as good as they can be and being attentive enough to spot potential problem areas that can create havoc in the future. Maybe one person's weakness is in their competence, whereas another person's is in care. The point is that especially for the service leader, it's crucial that all 12 dimensions get treated with due attention.

I will also add that some people view leadership by looking at the top, where the great leaders are already standing. This is easy because leaders by definition are prominent and at the heart of the action. Instead, I suggest looking around for opportunities to lead – there are always vacuums waiting to be filled, waiting for us to come along and take the initiative. So don't look at the top of the pyramid for opportunities to lead – that time has come and gone. Instead, in the Service Age, the opportunities to lead surround us. Being competitive in the Service Age means being ready to step forward when the opportunity knocks.

ACTION!

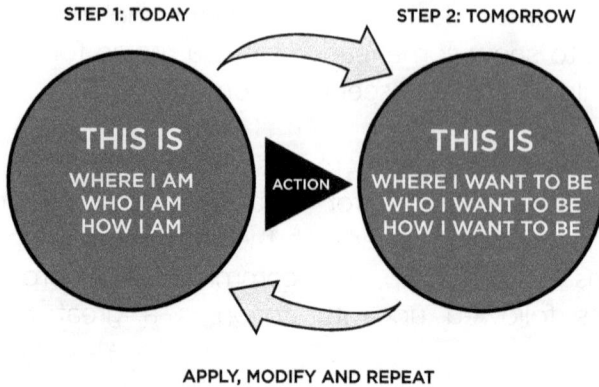

STEP 1: TODAY

STEP 2: TOMORROW

THIS IS
WHERE I AM
WHO I AM
HOW I AM

ACTION

THIS IS
WHERE I WANT TO BE
WHO I WANT TO BE
HOW I WANT TO BE

APPLY, MODIFY AND REPEAT

Review your *Leader : Follower* dimension and decide if it needs strengthening. The best way to assess whether or not you are strong in this dimension is to judge how effective you have been at bringing a genuine level of Competence, Character and Care into what you do. This dimension, as much or more than any other, is one that must continuously and conscientiously be reviewed and improved. The 'work' of being a good leader is an urge and commitment to building and maintaining trust, requiring self-reflection and ongoing improvement. Your ability to convey Competence, Character and Care will be reviewed and witnessed by those around you and this level will attract or repel others. In the context of the 12 dimensions, a leader's effectiveness is not expressed by how he or she commands but how he or she is able to organize action and decision-making as extensions of their trustworthiness.

Step 1: TODAY

Get a clear sense of your present situation. Write down the elements of your *Leader : Follower* dimension that affect where and how you live, work, and have fun in the different environments of your day-to-day world. This is what you're good at, what excites you and make you tick, as well as the behaviors and personal qualities that you would like to change.

1. _____

2. _____

3. _____

4. _____

5. _____

Step 2: TOMORROW
Make an inventory of what you would like to be in the future.
Although *Tomorrow* can literally mean tomorrow, it can also
mean one or five years from now.

1. _____

2. _____

3. _____

4. _____

5. _____

Step 3: ACTION
**Decide what you need to do to move from *Today* to
Tomorrow.** Define and carry out all actions great and small to
help move toward your goal.

1. _____

2. _____

3. _____

4. _____

5. _____

Step 4: APPLY, MODIFY, AND REPEAT

TOP CHEF IN ACTION – THE *LEADER : FOLLOWER* DIMENSION

One of the best things Sharon did when she was in the early stages of developing her business was to join the local branch of a business owner's association. Not only was it great for networking and exchanging with her peers, but it also helped her face the question of leadership head on. It was during one of their workshops that she realized she needed to change her thinking about what it was to be a business leader.

Although Sharon had been on the receiving end of different management styles, it wasn't until she launched the restaurant that she appreciated how challenging and rewarding it was to be in charge of its survival. She quickly realized that the only way she would be able to meet deadlines, fulfill expectations and keep the team together was by building the right team, delegating effectively, trusting in the competence of others, and earning her people's trust. She appreciated that if her team was to shine, they should all be empowered to make decisions and carry them out as needed.

She was especially sensitive to the importance of creating the right service conditions for everyone to succeed. From the start, she knew that earning and keeping her people's trust was critical, and she made it clear that even if people made mistakes, it could be constructive, and not destructive, if everyone learned from the experience.

To succeed, she convinced one of her previous instructors to act as her mentor, learning from his experience on what it takes to create and maintain a winning, top-quality restaurant. Through this mentor, the most important lesson she learned was to embody the qualities that she sought to deliver through the restaurant, starting with her own character.

Chapter
FIFTEEN

The *Life-long Learning : Maturation* Dimension

Chapter Summary:
This dimension is about staying on a path of learning and constantly upgrading your knowledge and skills to reinforce your relevance. Someone committed to lifelong learning and maturation will always remain useful to his or her network.

This dimension contains your commitment to continuously improve your education and knowledge, as well as maintaining a constructive attitude about who you are and what you can do. The learning process began when we were young, and by young I mean newborns. People are learning animals; we either do it passively, or we consciously make it a priority. Anyone who wants to make it as a service leader must keep learning and maturing. From the moment that we're born right until we're done with school (no matter what academic path we've taken), we will be more competitive if we remain active learners. For many, the learning momentum fizzles away once they're on the job. Other than the training and daily upgrades needed to keep their jobs, most people stop being active learners after graduation. This is unfortunate, because in order to be ready for the next promotion, we should always expand our knowledge and understanding of how things work to act with greater skill and maturity. Also, someone with new knowledge or information within a group tends to attract more people than someone saying the same old thing in the same old way.

I once caught up with an old schoolmate after several decades of not seeing one another. He had moved back from living in London and during our lunch he almost bragged that he hadn't changed much from who he was 30 years ago. My response was that he wasted three decades of his life. That's 30 years of stagnation. He blushed when he realized he had just admitted spending so long in a rut without growing. While the rest of the world was changing and moving on, he was still holding on to ideas that were probably outdated.

Remember that people turn to us for our unique brand of personal service. If we keep upgrading ourselves through lifelong learning as we mature, we will always be able to help people around us in increasingly profound ways. This means we stay relevant and interesting to the people around us. It's a great way to stay ahead of the pack. There's no better way to increase our social currency and ability to contribute to our groups.

Reviewing and improving your dimension doesn't need to come from constantly enrolling in new courses at school, although schools provide a convenient way to get intensive blasts of new ideas. You can also learn through hobbies and passions.

The point isn't about getting more information. We're in an age when information is commoditized – Google and other search engines have made information almost immediately accessible and literally at our fingertips. Instead, the point is to commit to always being in a state of learning as a path to making yourself a better service leader. This lifelong learning can come through formal or informal education, like getting greater professional status or accolades. Executives, for example, in order to be more competitive and useful for their companies, will often sign up for EMBA studies. This satisfies board requirements and helps round out how they contribute to their company's success.

As with the other dimensions, remember that in the service setting of our social networks, the people we serve aren't paying us with money but with respect, support and psychic rewards.

Most training and job-related learning is usually covered by companies during the first year or two. After that, companies may introduce more specialized training around specific systems, like with the implementation of a new software system or hardware. Beyond that, employers may support their people by training managers and above to be better managers and leaders, often bringing in consultants or professional coaches and trainers. Good companies certainly see the benefits of bringing in people to upgrade staff skills, but one shortcoming is if the training is purely functional, or remains rooted in the manufacturing mindset. Not that this isn't necessary or beneficial, but it misses out on so many other dimensions.

In cases where someone has been in the same role for many years without progressing, some introspection followed by action may be in order. Not being promoted is not in itself a warning sign - for example, you could be a perfectly happy and rewarded service provider who has found their bliss at work. However, if the feeling of stagnation has been setting in, there may be a few areas worth exploring. First, in terms of your habitat, maybe you're just not in the right role or company. Some companies may not have the interest or capacity to let their people progress in their careers. However, I take it as a warning sign if the company has horizontal operational diversity and you haven't had the opportunity to move across the organization. Companies that support their people to constantly upgrade and improve themselves understand the value that such investment pays off down the line. I expect these are the companies that attract and retain people for longer.

In some careers, lifelong learning is promoted by the sector itself. For example, physicians and accountants have to get a base number of annual CPD (continuous professional education) points, ensuring that they are up-to-date on important developments in their field. If your field or profession doesn't have a CPD program, or if learning through books isn't your style, then I suggest finding a mentor. Better still, find a 'master' and follow them as their 'apprentice'. More than mentors, the master-apprentice model is great for conveying practical in-the-field know-how. Mentors and masters are everywhere. In fact, anyone on the path to learning has to be open to or actively engaged with mentors and masters. Learning is a big part of personal development and maturation, and this often requires connection to others who will inspire or influence our learning paths. Mentors and masters have been in the trenches themselves and are a great source of information on shortcuts, dead-ends and false starts. They're great because they can be your active, personal advisor, which can make all the difference if you're in a crisis and need some outside perspective. Also, most people enjoy the role of mentoring. No matter how wise or rich their status, a mentor can give you a world of good in just five minutes – it's a great way to jump ahead.

A great example of someone dedicated to lifelong learning is the business leader and daytime television legend Oprah Winfrey. She started out from humble beginnings but by being conscientious about her own lifelong learning and self-management, she remains one of the most successful businesswomen in the world to this day. Take inspiration from Oprah, or anyone else to find the path for expanding your education. If you remain mindfully persistent, the result will be that you are increasingly seen as a valuable source of ideas within your network.

This dimension is about maintaining your curiosity about the world, your organization and other groups, and yourself. It's about always being aware that the world of what you know is dwarfed by the world of what you don't know. Tapping into this world of the unknown is where you will find personal and professional growth, and how you can always remain a valued member across all your relationships and groups.

There is an element within this dimension that really shouldn't be overlooked, which relates to what is sometimes called humility, as well as its opposite of arrogance or hubris. By humility, this is what feeds the maturation anyone must develop if they want to succeed as a great service leader or decent human being. Hubris is the arrogance you get when success goes to your head, having inflated your sense of accomplishment or expertise to the point that you stop being sensitive to those around you. If we look at truly great leaders, no matter what area of human activity, those who inspire and remain a benchmark for others are the people who showed humility even when they had every reason to celebrate their own importance. In service or leadership, and certainly to enhance your personal brand, your power and ability to influence will greatly expand as you show people around you that you are always open to being wrong, corrected or the chance to learn. This openness to others' ways of thinking, ideas and wisdom – no matter what their position in life – is the hallmark of a mature and inspiring service leader.

From the perspective of the Anna Karenina Principle, it's in a service leader's best interest to keep staying relevant through active learning. Not being up-to-date could mean missing out on even a small detail that proves to be life-threatening for the company or the job. A blind spot in this dimension could prove fatal.

ACTION!

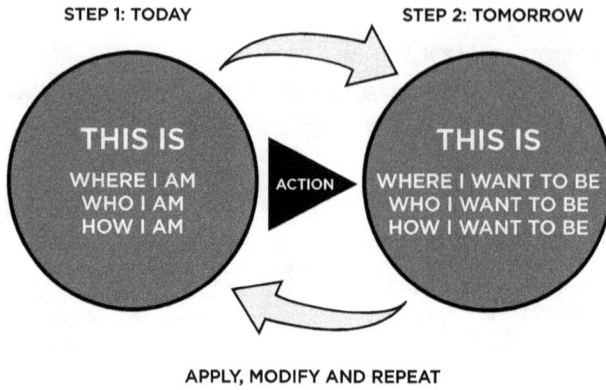

STEP 1: TODAY — STEP 2: TOMORROW

THIS IS
WHERE I AM
WHO I AM
HOW I AM

ACTION

THIS IS
WHERE I WANT TO BE
WHO I WANT TO BE
HOW I WANT TO BE

APPLY, MODIFY AND REPEAT

Anyone interested in greater levels of influence and success through service leadership must ensure this dimension is healthy and strong. It can't be said enough that if you want to be the best service leader you can be, learning and maturing are continuous, life-long pursuits. Completing this book is itself an expression of your *Life-long Learning : Maturation* dimension. To review this dimension, some reflection followed by specific action can help you maintain the growth associated with maturation. Needless to say, this dimension helps you review all your 12 dimensions across your professional and personal life, so that each day you refine the quality of how you connect with others.

Step 1: TODAY

Get a clear sense of your present situation. Write down the elements of your *Life-long learning : Maturation* dimension that affect where and how you live, work, and have fun in the different environments of your day-to-day world.

1. _____

2. _____

3. _____

4. _____

5. _____

Step 2: TOMORROW
Make an inventory of what you would like to be in the future.
Although *Tomorrow* can literally mean tomorrow, it can also mean one or five years from now.

1. _____

2. _____

3. _____

4. _____

5. _____

Step 3: ACTION
Decide what you need to do to move from *Today* to *Tomorrow*. Define and carry out all actions, great and small, to help move toward your goal.

1. _____

2. _____

3. _____

4. _____

5. _____

Step 4: APPLY, MODIFY, AND REPEAT

TOP CHEF IN ACTION – THE *LIFE-LONG LEARNING : MATURATION* DIMENSION

Sharon understands that in order to maintain the reputation of *Le Petit Plat*, she must always stay connected to what's happening in the industry. This isn't about changing with the seasons or following the latest food fashion, but about staying relevant. Her ultimate dream is to have the restaurant stable enough for her to go on 'sabbatical' – Michelin style.

While she was working in a Michelin-starred Parisian restaurant, she was surprised to meet a cook on the line who himself owned a Michelin-starred restaurant in Cambridge. He was spending a few months working next to Sharon in order to learn new techniques and recipes.

Sharon then found out that many top-chefs do this. Not only did she want to be able to take the time off to do this kind of cooking sabbatical, but she knew that in order to pull it off she needed to establish *Le Petit Plat* as a leading restaurant. For that to happen, she would need to continuously learn more, refine and improve the quality of the dishes that came out of her kitchen, and keep getting better as a business leader.

As a side project, she committed to spending four weeks per year in Vietnam, sitting with local chefs and learning new skills. Although quite different from the dishes she would offer back home, it helped broaden her abilities that she would then take to her team. From there, Sharon was inspired to find unknown Vietnamese recipes, elevating them to a new culinary level and publishing them in a new cookbook.

Chapter
SIXTEEN

The Conscientious Service Leader

I am convinced that committing to the goal of improving our skills as service leaders is critical in the Service Age. Not only will this facilitate our competitiveness and likelihood for success, but the result will also be that we support the people in our lives so that they themselves succeed in their lives. The 12 dimensions of the service leader described here provide a comprehensive checklist, all of which will strengthen your 3-Cs of Competence, Character and Care.

In the worst-case scenario, if you've tried to improve a few dimensions – the obvious ones – while ignoring other dimensions, you risk missing out.

In case remembering all the dimensions is impractical, you can use the shortcut of the 3-Cs to help keep you on track. Then, I suggest you keep this book for future reference. As long as you first go through an honest audit of your 12 dimensions, plan and execute your path to minimize the little faults that could bring you down, and then keep the spirit of the 3-Cs alive and well, you will stay on track to emerge as a great service leader.

Sustained success and excellence in the Service Age demand a strong, multidimensional service leader. By reviewing, improving and maintaining your 12 dimensions, and remaining a conscientious service leader who is curious about the world and always learning, you will provide the best personal service to the people in your life, no matter where they are in their own entrepreneurial journey.

Ran and I bid you great success as you dream big and move ahead on your own entrepreneurial journey. May you enjoy the many rewards that will come from true service leadership.

Acknowledgements

"Life is an entrepreneurial journey," my father told me when I was young. With that in mind, I have always wanted to share what I have learned and earned with future leaders. I extend my heartfelt thanks to Ran Elfassy for his contribution and commitment to this book by putting my ideas and thoughts into text. I am grateful for Willde Ng and his team at ThinkingWithoutThinking for the chic book-series design.

I will extend my heartfelt gratitude to the fabulous support team, namely Shela Chan, Mary Cho, Fanny Sze and Alice Yuen, for their dedication and support to the success of this book. Also in this list, I thank Arthur Bell, Peter Chan, Dexter Cheng, Hak Kin Choi, Francis Lo and Kingsley Smith.

I would also like to thank Victor Fung, Tom Osgood, Daniel Shek, Kai Man Wong, Linda Wong and the Principal Investigators of Service Leadership Initiative: John Burns, Kin Man Chan, Mark Hayllar, Reza Hoshmand, Ting Chuen Pong, Robin Snell and Kar Ming Yu.

Many thanks to you all.

Po Chung

I first met Po in 2006. I didn't know his history with DHL or his impact on Hong Kong and beyond. All I knew was that my gut told me he was a decent, thoughtful and deeply moral guy. I am thankful for having been able to join him on his entrepreneurial adventure.

I thank my parents, Alice Sadoun and Meir Elfassy, who supported me and helped me develop into the adult who would make the world his oyster. The foundation they set is everything on which everything else stands.

My gratitude to Delian is complete and everlasting. This book couldn't have happened without her support.

To everyone else who has influenced my 12 dimensions, I am grateful for each step and minute we've shared together.

Ran Elfassy

Bibliography

1. *"Google Core Values"*. Blogoscoped. 2007-01-25. Retrieved 2013-06-14.

2. Kouzes James M., Posner Barry Z.; *The Leadership Challenge: How to Make Extraordinary Things Happen in Organizations*; Jossey-Bass; 3 edition (August 7, 2003)

3. Carnegie, Dale; *How to Win Friends & Influence People*; Pocket Books (October 1, 1998)

4. Chung, Po and Ip, Saimond; *1. THE FIRST 10 YARDS - The 5 Dynamics of Entrepreneurship and how they made a difference at DHL and other successful startups;* Cengage Learning Asia (December 19, 2008)

5. Gad, Thomas; *Branding: Cracking the Corporate Code of the Network Economy, Financial Times/Prentice Hall (December 29, 2000)*

6. Diamond, Jared; *Guns, Germs, and Steel: The Fates of Human Societies*; W. W. Norton & Organization (April 1, 1999)

7. Marcuse, Herbert; *One-Dimensional Man: Studies in the Ideology of Advanced Industrial Society*; Beacon Press (October 1, 1991)

8. Stickdorn, Marc and Schneider, Jakob; *This is Service Design Thinking: Basics, Tools, Cases*; Wiley; 1 edition (January 11, 2012)

9. Pirsig, Robert M.; *Zen and the Art of Motorcycle Maintenance: An Inquiry into Values*; William Morrow Paperbacks (September 30, 2008)

10. Magretta, Joan (Author) and Stone, Nan (Contributor), *What Management Is: How It Works and Why It's Everyone's Business*; Free Press; 1 edition (April 30, 2002)

11. Levene, Malcolm and Mayfield, Kate; *10 Steps to Fashion Freedom: Discover Your Personal Style from the Inside Out*; Harmony (April 24, 2001)

12. Lyubomirsky, Sonja; *The How of Happiness: A New Approach to Getting the Life You Want*; Penguin Books; Reprint edition (December 30, 2008)

13. Csikszentmihalyi, Mihaly; *Flow: The Psychology of Optimal Experience*; Harper Perennial Modern Classics; 1ST edition (July 1, 2008)

14. Newport, Cal; *So Good They Can't Ignore You: Why Skills Trump Passion in the Quest for Work You Love*; Business Plus (September 18, 2012)

15. Kahneman, Daniel; *Thinking, Fast and Slow; Farrar*, Straus and Giroux (April 2, 2013)

16. Newport, Cal; *Deep Work: Rules for Focused Success in a Distracted World; Grand Central Publishing (January, 2016)*

www.ingramcontent.com/pod-product-compliance
Lightning Source LLC
Chambersburg PA
CBHW060022210326
41520CB00009B/962